Azura Othman

Towards a Sustainable Fiscal Position for Malaysia

De Gruyter Studies in Islamic Economics, Finance and Business

Edited by
Abbas Mirakhor and Idris Samawi Hamid

Volume 11

Azura Othman

Towards a Sustainable Fiscal Position for Malaysia

A Proposal for Reform

DE GRUYTER

ISBN 978-3-11-058779-1
e-ISBN (PDF) 978-3-11-059118-7
e-ISBN (EPUB) 978-3-11-058802-6
ISSN 2567-2533

Library of Congress Control Number: 2021943078

Bibliographic information published by the Deutsche Nationalbibliothek
The Deutsche Nationalbibliothek lists this publication in the Deutsche Nationalbibliografie; detailed bibliographic data are available on the Internet at http://dnb.dnb.de.

Cover image: nnnnae/iStock/Getty Images Plus
Typesetting: Integra Software Services Pvt. Ltd.
Printing and binding: CPI books GmbH, Leck

www.degruyter.com

Preface

Over the past three decades, the Malaysian economy has undergone a growth paradox; on one hand experiencing growth, while at the same time witnessing deterioration of overall fiscal balance and consequently a rise in national debt. Being an open economy, Malaysia has had its fair share of instability, mostly as a result of contagion effects of regional and global crises. However, having a stable government and judicious policy stance had allowed the country to resume its growth path in post-crises period. Malaysia is a well established middle-income country that aspired to achieve a high-income status by 2020. Like most emerging markets, large and growing public debt, volatile commodity prices, creeping corrupt practices and policy incoherence due to recent changes in government had imposed a constraint on achieving its target within the envisioned timeline. The onset of a worldwide pandemic in 2020 had further hampered this quest. Policy reforms recommended in this book could well allow Malaysia to regain the high-income trajectory.

As a country that has faced persistent fiscal deficits for the past 22 years, Malaysia now needs more fiscal space and a plausible fiscal sustainability plan that would place its economy on a trajectory towards a higher growth path. Its budget deficit in 2020 stood at 5.8% of GDP while federal government debt stood at more than 60% of GDP. Even though recent reports have indicated an easing of the country's budget deficit in the years to come, the current subdued global growth may not place Malaysia in a balanced budget position in the near future.

One of the main challenges to reform the current policy structure is steering out of the "path-dependency" created by elements of interest ingrained in the financial system. This book is dedicated to exploring a new path that builds on the foundational principles of risk sharing Islamic finance. The moral dimension to risk sharing is its ability to strengthen social solidarity by enhancing cooperation amongst all economic agents. Public policy plays an important role in creating an effective incentive structure to promote risk sharing, which requires transparency, high level of trust and good governance amongst economic players.

Against this backdrop, this book assesses the sustainability of Malaysia's current fiscal position. At the same time, it looks at the viability of an alternative fiscal framework based on a flat tax system and interest-free public financing that involves extensive public participation. Based on financial data of the Malaysian government from the years 1970 to 2013, a simulation of a new tax revenue stream and a federal government liability position under the proposed policy configuration are generated. With the use of a fiscal sustainability indicator and fiscal sustainability test, the fiscal sustainability position of the existing and proposed fiscal framework for Malaysia is assessed. The fiscal sustainability test involves testing for unit root and cointegration of government revenue and expenditure, as well as the error correction model to analyse the relationship of the two fiscal variables. Using Dynamic

https://doi.org/10.1515/9783110591187-202

Ordinary Least Squares, the author evaluates the viability of the proposed fiscal policy framework vis-à-vis the existing fiscal framework in the context of providing a more sustainable fiscal position for Malaysia.

Based on the research, the existing fiscal position of Malaysia shows wavering sustainability, but the newly proposed fiscal reform shows a strong sustainability position. If implemented, it would reduce public debt burden, strengthen fiscal policy, increase financial inclusion, reduce income and wealth disparities, and achieve a resilient high-income economy. This is the book's proposal for an alternative fiscal policy structure for policymakers.

Contents

1 Introduction

Post-Asian financial crisis in 1997/1998, Malaysia began to record budget deficits after a five-year period of budget surplus. Being an open, developing economy with worldwide trade partners, the contagion effect of the financial turbulence that has hit the world economy in recent years has hampered Malaysia's effort to improve its fiscal situation and pull itself out of the grips of fiscal imbalance. The onset of a worldwide pandemic in late 2019 has further dampened the recovery effort.

Amid concerns of a persistent fiscal deficit, Malaysia has taken steps to consolidate its fiscal position. The measures taken by the government thus far – mainly in the form of subsidy rationalization and the introduction of the Goods and Services Tax (GST) in 2015 – although necessary, had not been popular among the masses. The adverse effects of said measures on the price level of goods began to develop immediately after its implementation. Changes in government policies due to changes in government since 2018 saw the GST being repealed in 2018. Although the abolishment of GST was a welcomed change to consumers, but to the government, it has to be balanced by a review in planned government spending to check for leakages and to supplement the reduction in revenue.

However, the adverse impact of the pandemic on the economy has necessitated the government to provide financial assistance to those affected by closure of businesses due to lockdowns, which had to be financed by borrowing. Increased borrowing via bond issuances or long-term government borrowing is also not a desirable solution, as interest payments will impose a burden on future taxpayers. Reintroduction of the GST has also been mooted as a measure to increase government revenue. Additionally, growing uncertainty has arisen about the adequacy of current policy regimes that are anchored on the interest-based debt system to provide a sustainable solution to economic stability.

Whether or not current measures will achieve the desired results depends on many factors. For example, an increase in tax revenue through consumption tax is not likely to improve its fiscal position if the government does not reign in its operating expenditure and borrowing. Additionally, the impact of consumption tax on domestic consumption and inflation, and the knock-on effect on the economy, may not augur well with the current pandemic situation. In this book we aim to present an analysis of Malaysia's current fiscal position and explore an alternative fiscal framework that may improve Malaysia's fiscal sustainability.

1.1 The Status Quo

It is important for policymakers to determine the sustainability of the current fiscal policy stance as this may indicate the need for policy correction. Studies have also

https://doi.org/10.1515/9783110591187-001

shown that high debt levels impair growth.[1] The current government borrowing level in Malaysia has breached its cap of 55% of GDP per the Government Funding Act 1983. In 2020, this threshold was increased to 60% as a temporary measure to soften the impact of the Covid-19 pandemic on the Malaysian economy. If the contingent liabilities of the government, which is not immediately evident in financial reporting, are taken into account, the percentage of debt to GDP would be significantly higher than reported. A high level of debt constrains the government's ability to take on additional risk in its balance sheet. Persistent fiscal deficits also impair the effectiveness of policymakers in responding to future shocks. Additionally, there has been adverse distributional impact from increasing debt burden – especially when the borrowing is not for financing future development. This affects both present and future generations. This is because the middle- and lower-income classes carry the burden of the taxes required to service the government debt, which is held by either higher income groups or foreign investors. This distributional impact will further contribute to the divergence in the income inequality that is already present in Malaysia, as evidenced by the high Gini index of 41% in 2019.[2]

The government appears to be making populist pledges and contributions at the expense of deteriorating public finances. In order to continue doing so, the government has to find alternative sources of revenue that will counter the current increasing debt position. The country also cannot perpetually rely on oil revenue. The reduction in the percentage of budget deficit over the last few years prior to the onset of the Covid-19 pandemic, may place Malaysia on track towards a balanced budget position, but the speed of recovery is contingent upon the growth rate of the economy. In the meantime, the government's subsidy rationalization measures in the last decade adversely impacts 80% of the population who are from the middle to lower income group. Price hikes of certain essential items as a result of that action will reduce the purchasing power of this segment of the population. As lower income groups tend to have a higher marginal propensity to consume, this could dampen domestic demand and drag the recovery process further.

There is therefore a need to study the country's present fiscal position, and its trajectory if no corrective measures are taken:

1. *Narrow tax base*: Statistics show that only about 8% of the 33 million Malaysian population are currently contributing to the country's tax revenue. In 2011, the Direc-

1 Reinhart & Rogoff, (2010) in the article "Growth in a Time of Debt" published by the American Economic Review (2010) found that the GDP growth of a sample of 44 countries declines with increasing debt.

2 Gini index as provided by the Department of Statistics Malaysia in the as reported by the Household Income and Basic Amenities Survey Report 2019 its website.

tor General of Inland Revenue was reported to have said that out of the 5 million people eligible to pay tax, only 1.7 million are active taxpayers.[3] The remainder are ineligible either because they are retired, have stopped working, currently enjoying tax benefits or have incomes below the tax threshold. The number of taxpayers is small compared to the workforce of 15 million individuals in Malaysia. This means that only a small portion of the Malaysian population is contributing towards the development of the country while the rest are beneficiaries of social services and utilities provided by the government. Considering the low percentage of the population contributing to the operation of the country, there is a perceived injustice created by the current tax system that must be addressed. Although the introduction of GST may have brought in the additional revenue to the government, it is at the expense of fair distributional outcome, as the tax will impact the poor and the wealthy alike.

2. *Complex tax structure*: The complexity of the tax legislation makes it difficult for taxpayers to both understand and comply. Taxpayers must not only know income tax laws and Public Rulings issued by the Tax Authorities but must also be familiar with their administrative practices to ensure that their tax returns are filed correctly and follow the correct timing and procedure. Taxpayers will normally have to engage tax consultants and tax executives to handle their tax matters, which adds to the cost of doing business. To further exacerbate the situation, such tax compliance cost is not recognised as a tax-deductible expense in computing the taxpayers' tax liability. The government also incurs costs in terms of resources for administrative work such as auditing the tax assessments made by taxpayers and collecting the correct amount of tax. Sometimes, resources have to be spent on defending contentious tax positions. Disputes may arise on the interpretation of tax legislations that require legal advice and involvement of the Court. Due to the complexities and loopholes in the tax legislation, some may choose not to comply, or find creative ways of shirking the tax system. Many of these problems may be resolved by adopting a simple taxation system.

3. *Tax leakage*: A complex tax system provides incentives for shrewd taxpayers to find loopholes in the law to avoid or reduce tax payments. At the same time, incidence of tax evasion further reduces tax revenue collection. In 2011, the Inland Revenue Board was reported to collect an additional RM22 billion (US$5.41 billion), representing a 27% increase in tax revenue compared to the previous year. The increase was said to be attributable to efforts taken to fight tax evasion. On the one hand, the amount collected signified an increased efficiency in tax collection; while on the other hand, it highlighted the presence of tax avoidance and evasion activities. Apart from plugging these tax leakages through special task forces, the window

3 Quoted by Inland Revenue Board Chief Executive Officer, Datuk Dr Mohd Shukor Mahfar, Borneo Post Online, 11 September 2011.

of opportunity to engage in such activities must be closed with a tax system that leaves little or no room for manipulation.

4. *Substantial cost of economic stimuli*: In March 2009, the government at the time, introduced and implemented an unprecedented RM60 billion (US$14.76 billion) stimulus package to help Malaysia weather the global economic crisis. This was in addition to a first stimulus package of RM7 billion (US$1.72 billion) previously announced. In the run up to the 2013 general election, the previous ruling government also distributed cash handouts and various other incentives to the lower-income sectors of the population as part of the Government's People's Aid program. The amount involved for the 2011 handouts came to RM2.6 billion and a promise of increased handouts in the subsequent years if the ruling party were to remain in power. These expenses required funding, and given the deficit position, it was likely that borrowing was taken to finance expenditures. If the money for the cash handouts had come from increased tax revenue, it would show that the government is not exercising a prudent counter-cyclical fiscal policy by spending the additional taxes it has collected instead of using it to manage its deficit position.

Ever since the Covid-19 pandemic hit the world over, Malaysian government had to take measures to weather the impact of the pandemic on the economy especially to those who lost their livelihood due to lockdowns. The various stimulus packages that have been introduced thus far are valued at RM305billion, and this had to be taken amidst existing fiscal challenges and slow economic gorwth. Even though the Malaysian economy has seen steady albeit nominal growth over the last few years, the rate of growth should be fast enough to keep pace with the rate of growth of its debt.

5. *High cost of borrowing to cover deficits*: As borrowing increases, more resources have to be allocated to debt servicing at the expense of embarking on productive development projects. Interest-based borrowings significantly transfer the risk from the lender to the borrower and the consequences are detrimental to the borrower. The prevalence of debt in the economy will lead to a divergence between the financial and real sector of the economy, weakening the resilience of the economy. This situation, coupled with persistent deficits, does not portend well for efforts by the government to preserve the country's sovereign rating. Additionally, debt servicing puts a strain on the economy when it is growing at a slower pace than the rate of interest.[4] External borrowing, on the other hand, results in an outflow of funds. The total external debt, including the private sector as of 2019 is RM946 million

4 An IMF study by Arcand et al. (2012) showed that finance starts to have a negative effect on output growth when credit reaches 100% of GDP regardless of output volatility or incidence of banking crises.

(RM747 million in 2014), which makes up approximately two thirds of the Gross National Income.[5]

6. *Deteriorating sovereign rating*: For the first time in many years, Fitch Rating had downgraded Malaysia's sovereign credit rating outlook from "stable" to "negative" in July 2013. This was due to the deterioration in public finance and the perceived weakening of prospects for fiscal consolidation and budgetary reforms. Another source of pressure on the credit profile is the rapid rise in government-guaranteed debt. Guarantees rose to 15% of GDP by end-2012 from 8% at end-2008.[6] Malaysia's current account surplus also declined from 17% in 2008 to 8% in 2012[7] driven partly by the drawdown of public sector savings as well as by increased investment. A lower rating means it will be more expensive for Malaysia to borrow externally. It will also dampen foreign investment flows in Malaysia's equity and bond market. Even though other international rating agencies such as Moody's and Standard and Poor's, have opted to maintain a "stable" assessment, the effect of the downgrade by Fitch could be felt by the sell down pressure of Malaysia's blue-chip shares and flight of foreign funds. The rating improved in subsequent years to A- stable and remained so until 2019 before the impact of the pandemic resulted in a downgrade of rating to BBB+ as of end-2020.[8] This points to the statement made earlier; that in a highly leveraged situation, Malaysia lacks fiscal space to manoeuvre in an unexpected economic downturn, hence a need for a holistic fiscal consolidation.

The issues highlighted above can be summarised into the following concerns that this book intends to address:
- Long-term sustainability of the economy
- Adequacy of tax revenue to cover government expenditure and perceived injustice brought about by the current tax system
- Adverse distributional impact arising from rising government debt

1.2 Sustainable Solutions

We propose a fiscal reform of the tax structure and public sector borrowing policy, and assessing its potential in improving the current deficit position to bring Malaysia towards a sustainable fiscal position.

5 BNM Annual Report 2015 and 2019 (Annex pg 13 and 8 respectively)

6 FitchRatings, Malaysia Budget Signals Reform, but Implementation is Key, 28 October 2013 (accessed from https://www.fitchratings.com/gws/en/fitchwire/fitchwirearticle/Malaysia-Budget-Signals?pr_id=806210 on 9 January 2014)

7 Sourced from Department of Statistics Malaysia.

8 Reported in Fitch Ratings official website https://www.fitchratings.com/entity/malaysia-80442213#ratings

Malaysia's budget deficits over the last twenty-two years have received increasing attention from economic observers, especially in terms of the effectiveness of current policy measures. Apart from the effect of the global economic crisis, imprudent expenditure management may also be a factor contributing to the fiscal deficit. The options open to fund the deficit are either to increase the revenue base or to increase borrowing through bond issuances. In this book, we provide policymakers with an overview of the sustainability of the current fiscal policy and an alternative fiscal policy structure that can better address the deficit situation. These reforms will potentially lead to a change in the design and implementation of fiscal and monetary policies.

The cornerstone of these reforms is its potential to emulate the characteristics of an ideal economy based on the Islamic worldview:
- Social justice and equity with more equitable distribution of income
- Trust and transparency
- Cooperation and coordination through sharing of risks
- Finance grounded in the real economy

Ultimately, the policies are aimed at achieving the essential attributes for the existence of a harmonious economy, especially for a pluralistic country such as Malaysia. This is because social solidarity is one of the prerequisites for human development, which in turn is closely tied to the development of a nation.

1.3 Impact of Policy Reform

Fiscal sustainability is about the ability of a government to sustain its current spending, taxes, and other policies in the long run, without threatening solvency or defaulting on some of its liabilities or promised expenditures. Therefore, policies which encourage an increase in tax revenue for the government and financial resource mobilization for the public sector without resorting to debt, is ideal.

As far back as ten years ago, the concern on the fiscal sustainability and its effect on economic growth if Malaysia does not rein in borrowing has been raised in the National Economic Advisory Council (NEAC) Report 2010 on the Malaysia New Economic Model. The report suggested a fiscal reform that focuses on the establishment of an efficient, simple and transparent tax system.

Studies thus far have focused on conventional approaches to fiscal and monetary adjustments to address imbalances in the economy (Alesina & Tabellini, 2005; Debrun & Kapoor, 2010; Moreno-Dodson, 2013; OECD, 2012; Perotti & Alesina, 1995; Perotti, 1999; Sutherland, Hoeller, & Merola, 2012; Wyplosz, 2012). Fiscal studies in Malaysia have examined the relationships between fiscal and macroeconomic variables (Y. K. Chen, 2012; George, 2012; Rafiq & Zeufack, 2012; Taha & Loganathan, 2008), and fiscal sustainability (Abdullah, Mustafa, & Dahalan, 2012). However, to the author's knowledge, there has been no empirical study on the impact of reforming the tax structure in Malaysia apart from a study on improving the efficiency of the tax system and the implementation of GST (Mansor, Tayib, & Yusof, 2005; Palil & Ibrahim, 2011; Zhou, Jarren, & Heng-Contaxis Jordon, 2013). There are also no studies focused on assessing alternative financing measures for the public sector, in particular mobilizing idle resources into productive use. Malaysia's private sector savings for the past five years had been in excess of RM300million, and gross national savings had been between 24% to 30% of the country's Gross National Income.[9] These funds represent untapped resources for financing public sector development activities and to ease the current constraints in the fiscal space. The book therefore aims to assess a new framework for public finances with two elements:

- A tax structure that can improve the tax revenue
- Public sector financing that mobilises non-debt-creating sources to finance development expenditure

Discourse on reforming the tax system is nothing new, but the steps taken have not been comprehensive enough to consider a simpler and more equitable tax structure. The aim of the reform in the tax structure is to increase tax revenue through greater tax compliance, while imposing a tax rate that is based on the financial capacity of the taxpayer. A flat tax system on income and wealth is simple as there will be only one rate of tax that applies to all and those are the only taxes to be levied. The imposition of tax on wealth provides additional revenue to the government, and most importantly it is imposed on the more able segment of the population. Income alone may not be a sufficient measure of wellbeing or taxable capacity. It is the possession of wealth that adds to the capacity to pay tax over and above the income it yields. Therefore, in the interest of equity, it is justifiable to tax wealth in addition to income. Wealth represents a wider tax base, enabling the rate of tax to be kept low.

The policy reform also suggests an interest-free public sector financing policy to circumvent the harms of interest-based borrowing. An interest-based financial system creates a divergence between the financial and real sector of the economy, as interest is payable notwithstanding thc outcome of the economic activities that the loan finances. A financing policy based on a system of risk sharing moves away from pure profit maximisation incentive and cultivates a system that is devoid of externalities, setbacks and pursuits of certain groups at the cost of others within the society. Under such policy the government's development expenditure will be financed through the issuance of risk sharing instruments in small denominations to the public. The partnership between government and the public in development projects will not only mobilise idle private savings in Malaysia to productive use, but will also allow for private savings – currently generating returns of 2% to 3%, to

9 Based on Bank Negara Annual Report 2020 (Annex pg 3)

a potentially higher return based on real-sector returns of the economy. The cost of raising financing to the government, via risk sharing instruments would not be much higher than the current rate of return paid on debt instruments. Instead, it provides a better impetus to the growth of the economy by mobilising idle funds.

We may need to look beyond the usual fiscal measures of increasing taxes and widening the tax base – regardless of ability to pay; and increasing interest-based borrowing – regardless of the distributional implications. It will be shown that Malaysia can benefit from the proposed policy reform in which:

- The burden of tax is distributed based on ability to pay
- There exist a more equitable opportunities to access the wealth of the nation, regardless of status, which in turn will further strengthen social solidarity
- The risk-sharing feature of public sector financing will forge a much closer connection between the country's financial and real sectors, thus imparting greater stability and resilience to the economy
- The burden of debt is no longer imposed on the taxpayers, and future generations are safeguarded from shouldering the debt of the current generation
- Financial inclusion among the majority of the people of Malaysia will be promoted

At the same time, the reform leads to positive distributional impact on income and wealth, and sharing of risk increases trust, transparency, cooperation, and coordination among the people and between the people and the government, which is an important element in preserving stability and strengthening social solidarity in a pluralistic country such as Malaysia.

2 Fiscal Policy and Sustainability

2.1 Introduction

Fiscal policy refers to adjustments in government spending and tax rates to influence the level of economic activity. Taxes, along with other government revenue and public sector borrowing, finance government spending. During periods of low growth and productivity where revenue is insufficient to fund government spending, public debt will be used to meet the shortfall. This is where fiscal management is critical. The level of debt has to be kept at a sustainable level in order to avoid a debt crisis. At the same time, government spending and tax structures must be set at a level conducive for stimulating economic growth.

The attention given to public debt and fiscal sustainability was previously focused on developing and emerging market economies. In recent years, rising debt levels have become a major concern for developed and industrialized countries. However, debt is not necessarily bad. This is evidenced by countries with high public debt but still record economic growth. Debt is sustainable as long as the rate of growth of the economy is higher than the rate of interest on debts taken. However, several financial crises in recent years have revealed an important insight which may have been taken for granted during the boom years; i.e. high debt increases the vulnerability of the economy to financial shocks.

One of the most important roles of the government is to design and implement incentive structures in government policies in order to guide the overall pace of the economy and maintain steady growth, high levels of employment and price stability. The two main policies used by the government to regulate the economy are monetary policy (effected through control of money supply and credit) and fiscal policy (effected through the control of spending and tax rates). The fiscal approach to macroeconomic consolidation involves the use of government taxes, spending, and borrowing to influence economic activity. In theory, any borrowing taken to finance shortfall in revenue is to be repaid by the subsequent growth. However, in the recent economic climate, more often than not the present and prospective rates of growth of the economy are not significant enough to validate debt levels, which in some cases exceeds 50% of the GDP. Judicious fiscal management is therefore important in order to ensure that the economy is resilient in the face of economic shocks.

2.2 Theoretical Foundation of Fiscal Policy

The use of either monetary or fiscal policy or a mix of both depends on the political orientations and philosophies of those in power at a particular time. Contemporary

https://doi.org/10.1515/9783110591187-002

fiscal policy is often based on the theories of the British economist John Maynard Keynes. Keynesian economics, as it is famously known, was developed in the wake of the Great Depression of the 1930s. Prior to the Great Depression, most governments approached economic matters with a *laissez faire* attitude, or free market economy with limited government intervention. As the prolonged unemployment of the 1930s remained unexplained, Keynes developed a theory that the unemployment of 1930s was a result of structural inadequacy in the economic system to move output and employment towards full employment levels. Keynes argued that the economy, left on its own, might lead to inefficient macroeconomic outcomes and allowing the market to self-adjust may be a lengthy and painful process. Hence, he advocated a role for government intervention in times of recession – by increasing government spending and reducing taxes – to stimulate the economy.

The side effect of such fiscal stimulus is normally an increase in budget deficit and government debt. As long as the rate of growth of the economy is higher than the rate of interest on debt, the fiscal position of a country may still be sustainable. Fiscal stimulus has to be introduced at the right time and with the right size and composition. There are three major reasons why fiscal policy sometimes does not achieve stability and growth as desired: Firstly, fiscal changes require legislative approval that takes time. Secondly, there is a time lag between the instituted change in fiscal policy and the impact exerted by the change. Thirdly, the time lags imply that sound policy requires knowledge of the economic conditions years into the future when the ability to forecast future conditions is limited.

Even though Keynes' theory was prominent in the post-World War II years, its dominance waned in the 1970s when it was unable to explain the simultaneous occurrence of high employment and inflation, also known as stagflation. However, the severe recession of 2007/2008 generated renewed interest in Keynesian analysis.

Fiscal policy can be carried out through automatic stabilisers or discretionary fiscal policy. Automatic stabilizers are changes in tax revenues and government spending that operates automatically as an economy moves through the business cycle. Discretionary fiscal policy refers to proactive action of the government to stimulate the economy through instruments of fiscal policy. Discretionary fiscal policy may be expansionary – in which the government increases its spending and/or reduces taxes to stimulate the economy; or contractionary, in which government spending is reduced and/or taxes are raised to slow down economic activities. Overall, fiscal policy is able to stabilise and smoothen the boom-and-bust economic cycle. The general view that fiscal policy should rely on automatic stabilisers as a stabilisation tool in an economic downturn was cast aside when countries around the world adopted fiscal stimulus packages to mitigate the impact of the financial crisis. This is based on the premise that monetary policy transmission mechanism would be less effective in a situation where considerable deleveraging is taking place. If fiscal policy has demand effects and shifts the demand for goods without crowding out private consumption, then there may be a role for countercyclical fiscal policy during recessions, as individuals and firms are more likely to be credit constrained. If the converse is true, then there is a role for pro-cyclical fiscal policy.

Generally, the aim of the government is to achieve a balanced budget whilst ensuring that the economy grows. A budget may not necessarily be balanced year-on-year. It can be cyclically balanced if it is balanced over the economic cycle; which means it can run a surplus in boom years and a deficit in lean years, with the surplus and deficit offsetting over time. To achieve this, fiscal prudence needs to be exercised in years when the economy generates fiscal surplus to cushion against any deficits during an economic downturn. If the budgetary situation necessitates borrowing, it has to be kept within the debt-servicing capacity of the economy. Such fiscal discipline will ensure sustainable macroeconomic stability and safeguard against vulnerabilities against unexpected adverse economic situations. This is in line with what Prophet Joseph or Yusof a.s. did when he foresaw in the dream of the King that seven lean cows ate seven fat cows. He interpreted the dream to mean there would be seven years of prosperity to be followed by seven years of famine.[10] As the appointed Minister of Finance of Egypt, he saved during the surplus years in anticipation of the deficit years.

2.2.1 The Common Pool Problem

Lack of fiscal discipline generally stems from injudicious use of policy discretion, leading to deficit bias. The deficit bias is explained by firstly, the tendency to push the discipline burden to future governments or future generations resulting in time inconsistencies of governments; and secondly, the interplay of the democratic processes and interest group politics. Politicians enhance their re-election probabilities by catering to interest groups and providing public largesse at the expense of future taxpayers (Wyplosz, 2012). Shifting the debt burden to future governments and spending above revenue capacity can be seen as a manifestation of the common pool problem. It has been generally accepted that the common pool problem arises when the recipients of public spending (or tax advantages) fail to internalise the costs that they impose on all other taxpayers.[11] Fiscal rules and independent fiscal institutions such as the Maastricht criteria are some of the solutions provided to address this issue but despite this, the high deficit phenomenon is prevalent in today's economic situation including developed nations. All the monitoring and

10 See Quran Chapter 12 (Yusof) Verses 43–49.

11 For a more detailed discussion on common pool problem in deficit bias and review of its solution, please see (Wyplosz, 2012).

rules put in place are to ensure that fiscal policy is sustainable and public debt levels in the long run does not threaten solvency.

2.2.2 Sustainability of Public Finance

The question of whether or not fiscal policy is sustainable has several implications. It will determine the need for future discretionary policy actions. Non-sustainable fiscal policy also involves the risk of a future increase in interest rates, leading to a slowdown in economic growth (Fernandez & Cos, 2002). Persistent fiscal imbalances or an unsustainable fiscal position may lead, sooner or later, to adjustments. Any fiscal adjustment involves cost, which depends on whether it is pre-emptive or forced by the market.

Delaying fiscal consolidation until such a time in which financial market confidence in the government deteriorates may increase the amount and cost of adjustment (Krejdl, 2006) and lead to unpopular measures. Hence, a sufficient lead in the signal of fiscal distress is important. Different choices of fiscal adjustment with equal magnitude may have different economic outcomes due to the multiplier effect of the different segment of the economy. For example, if the policy decision is to increase taxes, policy makers will have to consider which segment of the economy should be taxed more to produce the desired result in fiscal consolidation.

Considering the repeated occurrences of economic downturn and the fiscal consolidation measures taken that are sometimes lagging in effectiveness, it is worth considering the components of fiscal tools that are being used and consider their impediments. The answer to a more effective measure may lie in a more holistic reform to the fiscal policy stance. To illustrate this point, we will examine each fiscal tool and identify their impediments within the context of Malaysia's fiscal situation.

2.3 A Brief Overview of Malaysia's Fiscal Performance

Malaysia has a Fiscal Policy Committee (FPC) that takes a leading role in monitoring the fiscal position of Malaysia and strengthening public finances. The Ministry of Finance's Fiscal Policy Office, and an inter-agency technical group comprising officers from the Economic Planning Unit (EPU), Bank Negara and Ministry of Finance, supports the FPC. In Budget 2019, the Government mooted the Fiscal Responsibility Act to be tabled in 2021 aimed at institutionalising fiscal prudence, governance and transparency based on global best practices.

On May 2, 2009, the Prime Minister of Malaysia at the time announced the government's plan to develop a New Economic Model (NEM) that will expedite Malaysia's transition to a high-income country. The NEM emphasises ways to stimulate economic growth by increasing income and improving productivity of workers across all sectors of society. Other reforms include empowerment of the private sector and reduction in fiscal disparity between the wealthiest and poorest in Malaysia. In October 2019, the Government issued its Shared Prosperity Vision 2030, which is a commitment to make Malaysia a nation that achieves sustainable growth along with fair and equitable distribution, across income groups, ethnicities, regions and supply chain. Its aim is to provide a decent standard of living to all Malaysians by 2030. These strategic plans normally shape the budgetary requirements of the country, both in terms of taxation and government spending.

2.3.1 Government Debt and Deficit

In the mid-1980s, Malaysia experienced a major economic crisis, which was attributed to the poor performance of many state-owned enterprises, heavy external debts, depressed commodity markets and the overvalued exchange rate of the Ringgit. Pump-priming by the government in the early 1980s only resulted in increased budget deficits and public debt and a deferment of the crunch. The economy experienced a painful contraction in 1985 with negative GDP growth and widespread unemployment. The second economic crisis, which began in July 1997, was triggered by a sharp depreciation of the Malaysian Ringgit. The external value of the Ringgit fell by about 50%, while the Malaysian stock market plunged by nearly 60% (Ariff, 1998).

Except for a five-year period of surplus in mid-1990s, in the last two decades Malaysia has experienced episodes of budget deficits and carried one of the region's largest budget shortfalls in 2012 at 4.5%. Malaysia's main economic problem is the twin fiscal threat of fiscal deficit and rising debts. It has also done little to rein in public debt, which at that time officially lays only one percentage point under the debt-ceiling threshold of 55% of GDP. From 2013 onwards, save for 2017, the debt-ceiling threshold had been breached. Despite establishing committees to look into the deficit issue, the debt to GDP ratio continued to hover above the 55% threshold. In August 2020, the Government passed a legislation, Temporary Measures for Government Financing (Coronavirus Disease 2019 (Covid-19)) Act 2020, to allow the Government to provide funds to the economy in order to counter the impact of the Covid-19 pandemic. Apart from setting up the fund, the law will allow the government to raise the permissible statutory debt level ratio of 55% of GDP to 60%. The debt and surplus/deficit to GDP ratios relative to GDP growth for the last 20 years are shown in Figure 2.1.

During the period of stable GDP growth between 1990 and 1997, the debt to GDP ratio also declined while the budget ratio improved from a deficit to a surplus. The two dips in GDP growth from 1997 onwards represents the two major financial crises; the Asian financial crisis of 1998 and the sub-prime crisis of 2008/09. Even though GDP growth recovered close to the pre-1998 crisis levels, it did little to improve the budget deficit position. The debt to GDP ratio remained high, rising sharply from 39%

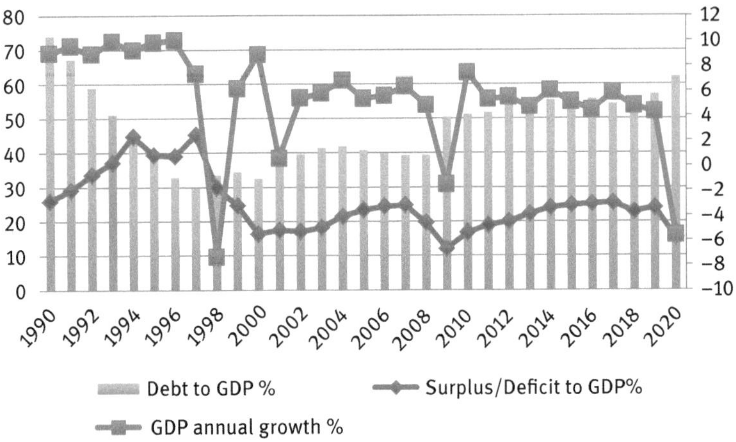

Figure 2.1: Debt and Deficit to GDP.
Source: IMF World Economic Outlook, October 2020, Tradingeconomics.

in 2008 to 50% in 2009 and continued to rise until 55% by the end of 2013. Thereafter, the budget deficit breached the 55% mark, and the dawn of the pandemic did not help to improve the situation.

Malaysia's rising Federal Government debts may not be the only problem of concern. There are also 'hidden' debts in the form of contingent liabilities such as government guarantees on private debt and 'off balance sheet' borrowings which is not reported as the Federal Government Debt. Contingent liabilities are difficult to trace and less transparent. Its existence may pose a higher risk than the official debt alone. In recent years, the government has increasingly issued debt papers via its statutory bodies and corporatized entities and provide guarantees to government-linked companies. The loans by these entities were obtained with guarantees provided by the Government but are not reflected as Federal Government borrowings. Subsequent to the change of government in 2018, reports of the government's "off-balance sheet" liabilities surfaced with the total government liabilities reported to be as high as RM1trillion.[12] If these contingent liabilities were included as government debt, the debt to GDP ratio would be well above 60% of GDP. This situation, if it were to happen in the Eurozone, would have sent the alarm bells ringing.[13] It is not inconceivable that these liabilities may eventually find their way on the Federal Government's balance sheet. The Accountant General of Malaysia has indicated

12 As quoted by the Ministry of Finance and reported by the The Edge Markets in September 2019, https://www.theedgemarkets.com/article/mof-defends-rise-direct-debt-under-ph-government.

13 The Maastricht Treaty signed by members of the European Union includes Maastricht criteria which among others the requirement for member countries to keep a deficit to GDP ratio of not more than 3% and debt to GDP ratio of not more than 60%.

that the Federal Government is in the process of transitioning the public sector accounting landscape from a modified cash flow basis to accrual accounting by 2015 to enable a more efficient and effective fiscal management.[14] With the change in basis of accounting, the official figure of debt to GDP ratio may be significantly different.

2.3.2 Government Expenditure

Examining the trend of income and expenditure over the last two decades in Figure 2.2, it may be surmised that Malaysia had been exercising pro-cyclical[15] fiscal policy where during the years 2000 to 2008, the increase in revenue was matched by a

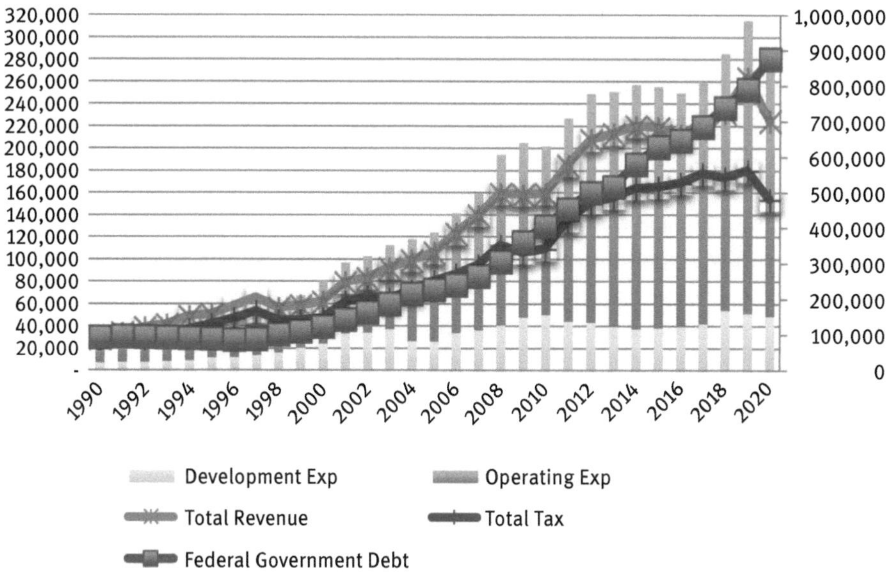

Figure 2.2: Government Debt, Revenue and Expenditure.
Source: BNM Monthly Statistical Bulletin January 2021.

14 The transition is part of public sector transformation under the New Economic Model. The adoption will put Malaysia public sector finance practice to be in line with the developed countries. This is based on presentation made at the Inaugural Treasury Economic Forum 2013 on 7 February 2013.
15 Procyclical fiscal policy is when spending goes up (or taxes go down) in booms and spending goes down (or taxes go up) in recessions.

corresponding increase in expenditure. This fact was also confirmed in a study by Rafiq & Zeufack (2012). Malaysia's revenue has enjoyed steady growth over the past two decades. However, as year-on-year total expenditure surpassed revenue, federal government debt increased by almost the same rate to make up the shortfall. In the span of 10 years, the government's debt has more than doubled (RM407 billion in 2010 to RM879 billion in 2020), outpacing revenue growth of only 41% during the same period (RM160 billion in 2010 to RM225 billion in 2020).[16]

After the sub-prime crisis of 2007/2008, the government announced a counter-cyclical measure in the form of two large fiscal stimulus packages which created a dent in the GDP growth in 2009 as shown in Figure 2.1.

The increase in government spending is attributable to the increase in operating expenditure such as emoluments, subsidies, supplies and services as can be seen in Figure 2.2. Figures 2.3 and 2.4 show the comparison of the component of government spending for the last ten years. The ratio of public servants to the overall population in Malaysia is almost 5%, which is one of the highest in the region. Naturally, remuneration of public servants is the biggest expense item on the budget. Development expenditure, which provides the potential for creating capital assets and future returns, has fallen over the years. The high operating expenditure also raises questions about the efficiency of the government sector in running the government administration. Instead of increasing efforts to keep its spending under check, the government has embarked on a deficit reduction exercise through reduction of government spending on subsidies, which currently accounts for 7% of total expenditure. This measure has hit the middle-income groups who do not qualify for the targeted subsidy programme such as the 1Malaysia People's Aid (BR1M) cash handouts.

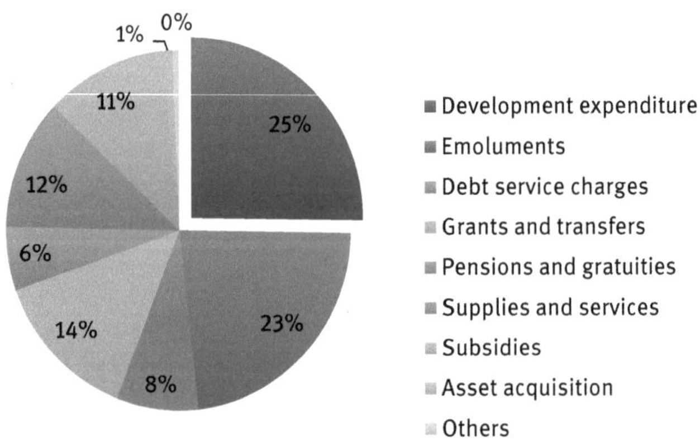

Figure 2.3: Composition of Government Expenditure 2010.

16 Based on Bank Negara Malaysia Statistical Bulletin January 2021.

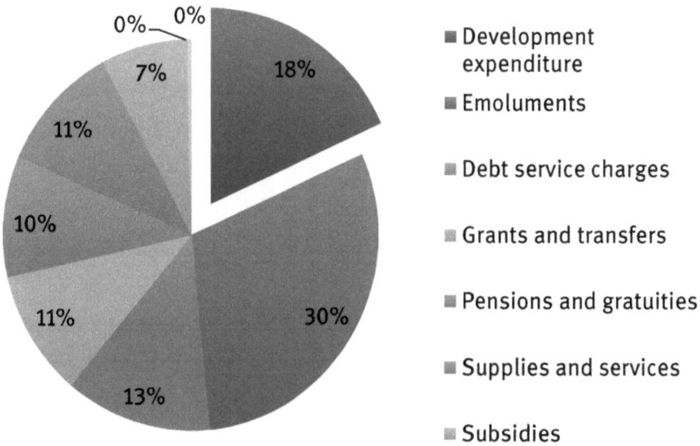

Figure 2.4: Composition of Government Expenditure 2020.
Source: Bank Negara Malaysia Monthly Statistical Bulletin January 2021.

2.3.3 Government Revenue

The Malaysian economy, save for the year of the financial crisis, has been enjoying a steady growth of nearly 5% year-on-year. Tax revenue is a major contributor of government revenue, yet the pool of taxpayers contributing to the government coffers is small. The size of the Malaysian population is approximately 32.5 million in 2019, of which 15.5 million makes up the total workforce. According to the Fiscal Outlook 2020 Report, only 16.5% of the 15.5 million workforces are eligible to pay tax.[17] The low number of taxpayers may be due to the existing tax structure, which provides too many exemptions or loopholes for tax leakage. Another reason is the middle-income status held by most Malaysians that puts the majority of the workforce below the tax threshold. This highlights a deficiency in the current tax system to capture the potential revenue. Nevertheless, due to improvement in efficiencies in tax collection such as the e-filing system and tax audits, the tax revenue collection has seen an increase since 2010. The government's revenue stream is heavily reliant on the state oil company Petronas, which is responsible for almost 40% of federal revenue.[18] As with other natural resources, this source of revenue may not be sustainable.

Direct taxes have been the more dominant source of revenue for the government as shown in Figure 2.5. With pressures mounting on the call for fiscal reform, the government has focused on broadening the tax base through the implementation of a new indirect tax, the GST. However, GST causes inflationary pressures that affects

17 Reported by The Edge Markets in October 2019, https://www.theedgemarkets.com/article/cover-story-budget-2020-top-tax-bracket-raised-30-tin-number-proposed
18 Retrieved from http://www.indexmundi.com/malaysia/economy_profile.html

The effectiveness of indirect spending in stimulating the economy depends on how well the incentives are being utilized by the private sector, or its multiplier[20] effect. On the other hand, the effect of government spending on goods and services can directly feed into the economy. However, to achieve maximum growth, the type of expenditure being undertaken should be developmental in nature – with the potential of creating higher aggregate demand as opposed to those that are operational in nature. This is because developmental projects such infrastructure has the potential to create new employment and national assets.

2.4.3 Government Borrowing

According to Keynesian economics, an increase in borrowing can be a stimulus to demand when other sectors of the economy are suffering from weak spending. Government borrowing is done through the issue of government debt or long-term government bonds. Government borrowing can benefit growth if it is used to finance capital spending that leads to an increase in the stock of national assets. This includes spending on transport infrastructure or educational facilities that improves the supply-side capacity and productivity of the economy. Debts, however, must be kept at a sustainable level to safeguard against solvency problem.

The following sections will explain in more detail the fiscal tools for Malaysia and identify their impediments in order to formulate an alternative policy structure.

2.5 Issues with Malaysian Fiscal Policy Tools

Two issues which need to be addressed in order to improve Malaysia's current fiscal scenario is the insufficiency of tax revenue and the high level of debt. Malaysia's tax structure has to be reformed to generate more revenue for the government and an alternative source of funds has to replace the current government borrowing.

Tax is the largest component of the Malaysian government's total revenue. There are various types of tax, the main ones being:

1. Income Tax
2. Real Property Gains Tax
3. Sales and Service Tax
4. Stamp Duty

Malaysia has been under the self-assessment system since 2000. This means that taxpayers have to self-assess their tax liability and the onus is on them to pay the correct

20 The multiplier effect depends on the marginal propensity to consume.

amount of tax. Heavy penalty provisions are imposed for under assessment of tax. As a check mechanism, tax audits are periodically conducted by the Inland Revenue Board ("IRB") to ensure that taxpayers have correctly assessed their tax liability. In addition to the various tax legislations, the IRB issues Public Rulings that provides guidelines and clarifications on how the provisions of the tax legislations have to be applied.

2.5.1 Income Tax

The current income tax system in Malaysia operates through a system of allowances and bands of income. Personal income tax is at various progressive rates ranging from 1% to 30% while the corporate tax rate is rather flat at either 17% or 24% in 2020. The tax rate has been on a declining trend ever since 2009 where the highest tax bracket used to be at 25%. However, since 2016, the rate has started to rise in the government's effort to collect more tax revenue. Which rate of tax and allowances are applicable depends on the status/nature and the residency of the taxpayer. The Income Tax Act, 1967 ("the ITA") governs the income tax legislation in Malaysia. Tax is levied on income accruing in or derived from Malaysia.[21] Section 4 of the ITA has classified the types of income that is subject to tax as follows:

1. Gains or profits from business
2. Gains or profits from employment
3. Dividends, interest or discount
4. Rents, royalties and premium
5. Pensions, annuities or other periodical payments
6. Gains or profits not falling under any of the foregoing

Unless specifically exempted (such as exemption on most interest income), non-resident individuals are also taxed on the income mentioned above, as well as other types of income specified under Section 4A of the Act (such as income from use of properties or installation of machinery, technical advice and rental of moveable property).

Resident individuals in Malaysia are taxed at a progressive tax rate and the tax rates (as at 2020) are as shown in Table 2.1.

Non-resident individuals, on the other hand, are taxed at a flat rate of 30%, while preferential rates of 15% is given to knowledge workers residing in Iskandar Malaysia in Johor. Those who work overseas and return to work in Malaysia are also liable to pay 15% flat rate for the first five years. Apart from resident individuals, cooperative societies are also taxed at a progressive tax rate, with different tiered rates than the above (Figure 2.2).

21 The exception to this derivation rule is for companies carrying on the business of banking, insurance, air transport and shipping, which are taxed on a world income scope basis.

Table 2.1: Personal Income Tax Rate (Resident Individual).

Chargeable Income (RM)	Tax Rate
Up to 5,000	0%
5,001 to 20,000	2%
20,001 to 35,000	3%
35,001 to 50,000	8%
50,001 to 70,000	14%
70,001 to 100,000	21%
100,001 to 250,000	24%
250,001 to 400,000	24.5%
400,001 to 600,000	25%
600,001 to 1,000,000	26%
1000,001 to 2,000,000	28%
Exceeding 2,000,000	30%

Table 2.2: Income Tax Rate for Companies.

Chargeable Income	Tax Rate
Resident company with paid up capital of RM2.5 million and below (or small and medium enterprise – SME)	
On first RM600,000	17%
Subsequent RM600,000	24%
Other resident companies	24%
Non-resident companies	25%

Certain preferential tax rates are given to insurance and Takaful companies (depending on type of business), approved operational headquarters companies, and foreign fund management companies. Therefore, different taxpayers are taxed at different rates depending on the nature of business and the level of income.

Statistics on the number of taxpayers in Chapter 1 show the presence of impediments in the current tax system. Apart from the narrow tax base, complexity of the tax system and tax leakages stated in Chapter 1, the progressive nature of the tax rates also pose several problems:

1. *Progressive tax system*: One of the main objectives of the progressive tax system is to reduce income inequality as it imposes a higher tax rate as income increases. In a progressive tax system, each additional ringgit is subjected to higher marginal tax rate. It builds on the idea that as income is a measure of someone's ability to pay, the higher income group should have a higher share of tax contribution to reduce income differences among taxpayers. The tax collected from the rich that is spent on welfare programmes for the poor narrows income differences. At first glance, a

progressive tax rate seems to improve equality. However, upon careful analysis, under certain tax environment and circumstances, a progressive tax rate may not achieve the desired outcome. Below are examples and illustrations of such situations.

Example 1: The Progressivity of Tax Declines with Deductions and Reliefs

The progressivity of marginal income tax rates across the income band is meant to impose larger taxes on the higher income group. However, the presence of tax deductions, reliefs and rebates reduces this progressivity simply because the tax savings from these deductions are proportional to the marginal tax rates – i.e. the higher the tax rates, the higher the deductions. Individuals are given various tax exemptions and rebates in arriving at the income chargeable to tax and the tax payable. Below are some examples:

Table 2.3: Personal Reliefs and Rebates.

Reliefs	Amount (RM)	Rebate	Amount (RM)
Personal	9,000	For chargeable income up to RM35,000	400
Husband/Wife (with no income)/ Alimony	3,000	Wife with no income	400
Child	2,000/8,000	Zakat	Up to the maximum of tax charged
Disabled child	6,000/8,000	Fee paid for employment pass	Full amount of fee paid
Life Insurance & EPF	7,000 (limited)		
Insurance premium for education and medical	3,000 (limited)		
Purchase of books, personal computer, sports equipment, etc	2,500 (limited)		

Similarly, companies are given various tax incentives in the form of tax exemptions (such as for pioneer status companies, Islamic fund management, etc.) and double tax deductions (such as for employment of handicapped employees, promotion of exports, etc.) in arriving at the chargeable income.

To illustrate this point, consider Mr. Low and Mr. High who earn RM48,000 and RM96,000 per annum respectively. Both have the same circumstances – they are both married, have a young child and claim no other reliefs apart from child relief and the maximum limit for life insurance and EPF. Therefore, the total relief for both of them is RM16,000. The taxable income is calculated based on the total chargeable income less the deductions received. Therefore, the calculation of tax payable for both of them is as follows:

Table 2.4: Illustration of Tax Savings from Deductions.

	Mr. Low (RM)	Mr. High (RM)
Total chargeable income	48,000	96,000
Less: Deduction of reliefs	16,000	16,000
Taxable Income	32,000	80,000
Tax Payable	510	6,700
Mr. Low (150 + 12,000@3%)		
Mr. High (4,600 + 10,000@21%)		
Average tax rate (with tax deduction)	1.1%	6.9%
Tax Payable (without tax deduction)	1,640	10,060
Average tax rate (without tax deduction)	3.4%	10.5%
Tax saving from deduction	1,040	6,160

In the above example, Mr. High who earns a higher income pays a higher tax. However, in terms of tax saving from deductions, Mr. High, who has double the income of Mr. Low, saves more from the deductions granted in absolute terms. The average tax rate for Mr. High is reduced by 3.6% whereas the average tax rate of Mr. Low is reduced by only 2.3%. Therefore, the exemptions give greater tax savings to higher income individuals than the lower income taxpayer, which then reduces the progressivity of the marginal tax rate.

Example 2: Progressive Tax Generates Less Revenue when the Majority of Taxpayers are in the Low and Middle-Income Group

Carrying on from Example 1, note that the total tax generated from two taxpayers earning RM48,000 is not equal to the total tax generated from one taxpayer earning RM96,000. Compare this with a situation where the taxable income is subject to a flat tax of say, 10%. The total tax generated from the two taxpayers earning RM48,000 will be equal to the total tax generated from one taxpayer earning the same total income, as illustrated in Table 2.5.

The above example also shows that the total tax collected under a progressive tax system is lower than that collected under a flat tax system, even though Mr. High pays at a rate which is 11% lower while Mr. Low experiences a 7% increase in tax rate. Currently about 60% of the Malaysian population is in the low to middle-income category; there is therefore a potential loss of tax revenue due to progressivity in the tax rate.

Table 2.5: Illustration of Total Tax Collected under Different Tax Regimes.

	Two of Mr. Low (RM)	One Mr. High (RM)
Progressive Tax		
Total Income	RM48,00 x 2 = 96,000	96,000
Tax Payable	1,640 x 2 = 3,280	10,060
Total Tax Collected		13,340
Flat Tax		
Tax Payable	48,000 x 2 x 10% = 9,600	96,000 x 10% = 9,600
Total Tax Collected		19,200

Example 3: Inflation disadvantages the lower income taxpayer under a progressive tax rate

Suppose at an inflation rate of 10%, the income of both Mr. Low and Mr. High in Example 1 rises to RM52,800 and RM105,600 respectively. The tax payable by both of them is now as shown in Table 2.6.

Table 2.6: Illustration of the Impact of Inflation.

	Mr. Low (RM)	Mr. High (RM)
Total chargeable income	52,800	105,600
Less: Deduction of reliefs	16,000	16,000
Taxable Income	36,800	89,600
Tax Payable	744	8,716
Mr. Low (600 + 1,800@8%)		
Mr. High (4,600 + 19,600@21%)		
Average tax rate	1.4%	8.3%
Increase in average tax rate	27%	20%

Under the current progressive tax rate in Malaysia, low and middle-income taxpayers suffer a higher increase in average tax rate in times of inflation. This is partly due to the structure of the tiered tax rates. The marginal tax rate for Mr. Low increases by 5% (8%–3%) more with the increase in income due to inflation, as inflation pushes Mr. Low into a higher tax bracket. However, Mr. High's marginal tax rate remains. Even with a further increase in income, this only pushes him to the next tax bracket by a 3% (24%–21%) increase. Note that as shown in Table 2.1, the incremental increase in the marginal tax rate between the income brackets is highest for the middle-income group, whereas the high-income group enjoys a smaller increase in marginal tax rates as they earn higher income (see Table 2.7).

The effect, as illustrated in the three examples above, may not be evident for companies as the corporate tax structure is rather flat. However, a similar argument

Table 2.7: Increase in Marginal Tax Rate Across Income Brackets.

Income Bracket (RM)	Marginal Tax Rate	Increase
5,001 to 20,000	1%	1%
20,001 to 35,000	3%	2%
35,001 to 50,000	8%	5%
50,001 to 70,000	14%	6%
70,001 to 100,000	21%	7%
100,001 to 250,000	24%	3%
250,001 to 400,000	24.5%	0.5%
400,001 to 600,000	25%	0.5%
600,001 to 1,000,000	26%	1%
1,000,001 to 2,000,000	28%	2%

may be applicable to the SMEs, who also suffer a 7% increase in marginal tax rates as their profits increase beyond RM500,000.

Example 4: Higher Marginal Tax Rates Encourage Tax Avoidance and Evasion

All taxpayers want to pay as little tax as possible to save more money, to spend, or invest. By nature, humans want as much disposable income as possible. Intuitively, the higher the marginal tax that a person must pay, the higher the incentive to avoid the tax, as each additional ringgit reported brings him closer to the next tax bracket. The incentive to avoid the tax does not only happen due to the progressivity of the tax rate. When a tax system is complex, there are more opportunities to find loopholes in the tax legislation to avoid tax. Different interpretations of the tax laws can also result in different tax outcomes. Sometimes this is done legitimately under the exercise of "tax planning". The higher income group has the means to do this by engaging tax experts and consultants to review transactions and structure them in such a way that minimizes the tax cost.

Suppose Mr. C is a single person and works as a senior manager in a firm. His salary package is RM120,000. As senior manager, he is entitled to stock option benefits. In order to reduce his tax liability, he has negotiated a salary package that comprises of an annual salary of RM100,000 and RM20,000 in stock options. Assuming the stock options were issued for free, a taxable benefit in kind arises from the said issue. However, the incidence of tax is deferred until the stock option is exercised.[22] Under this new salary package, Mr. C is able to reduce his tax liability as shown in Table 2.8.

22 An Employee Stock Option Scheme (ESOS) is a taxable benefit in kind to an individual. ESOS is taxable on the difference between the market value and the offer price of the shares at the date of offer of the option. The benefit is taxable upon exercise of the stock options but the tax liability of the benefit is related back to year the ESOS is issued.

Table 2.8: Illustration of Tax Planning of Salary Package.

	Tax Liability (without planning)	Tax Liability (with planning)
Salary	120,000	100,000
Less: Deductions	16,000	16,000
Chargeable income	104,000	84,000
Tax Payable	11,860	7,540

Using tax planning, Mr. C is able to reduce his marginal tax from 24% to 21% whilst still enjoying the same value of remuneration. At the same time, part of his tax liability (on the stock option) can be deferred. Even though all these actions are taken within the provisions of the tax laws, under the current progressive tax rates and rules, there are various ways of reducing tax liability. However, the incentive to avoid tax is balanced by the risk averseness of being caught and penalized for tax avoidance and evasion.

Based on the Household Income and Basic Amenities Survey Report 2019,[23] much of the growth in income in Malaysia is captured by the Top 20% (T20) of the population on a compounded annual growth basis. According to the report, the top 20 decile of Malaysians controls 47% of income in Malaysia. As the means to embark on clever tax schemes is high among the higher income group, the possibility of loss of income to the government is higher. As tax avoidance represents a leakage in government revenue, the use of a progressive tax system may undermine both the redistribution of income intended by this tax system and also the effort to increase revenue collection.

2. *Tax leakage*: Malaysia also suffers from tax leakages due to the use of complex offshore structures to gain tax advantages. A recent revelation by the International Consortium of Investigative Journalists in its Offshore Leaks Database[24] shows that many companies, including those in Malaysia, use offshore companies and complex tax planning to reduce taxes which are due to the government. This ties in with the points noted above; i.e. under high tax rates, taxpayers tend to find a lower tax jurisdiction to keep their income.

Additionally, it is the policy of the government to give tax incentives in the form of pioneer status company, investment tax allowance, reinvestment allowance and a host of other special exempt status and double tax deductions to promote certain sectors of the economy and to attract foreign investment. For example, the success of the development of the Iskandar Malaysia region in Johor has partly been

23 Household Income and Basic Amenities Survey Report 2020 accessed through the Department of Statistics Malaysia official website, www.dosm.gov.my

24 Accessed through http://www.icij.org/offshore/icij-releases-offshore-leaks-database-revealing-names-behind-secret-companies-trusts

attributable to various tax incentives granted by the government. Tax exemptions and incentives represent a loss of tax revenue to the government in the interim, which may be recouped in the form of higher income due to economic growth in the future. The question is whether the benefits given to recipients are ploughed back into the economy in the form of higher income and taxes. A snapshot of how tax revenue due to the government is lost is shown in Figure 2.6 where one can see how the tax system can create a divergence in income and wealth of the people. Large corporations and high-net-worth individuals (HNWIs) will naturally enjoy a higher bargaining power and financial might to take advantage of incentives or loopholes in the current tax system. The result is the rich will become richer and the poor will become poorer. The divergence in the income and wealth distribution if left to perpetuate, may eventually lead to social disorder.

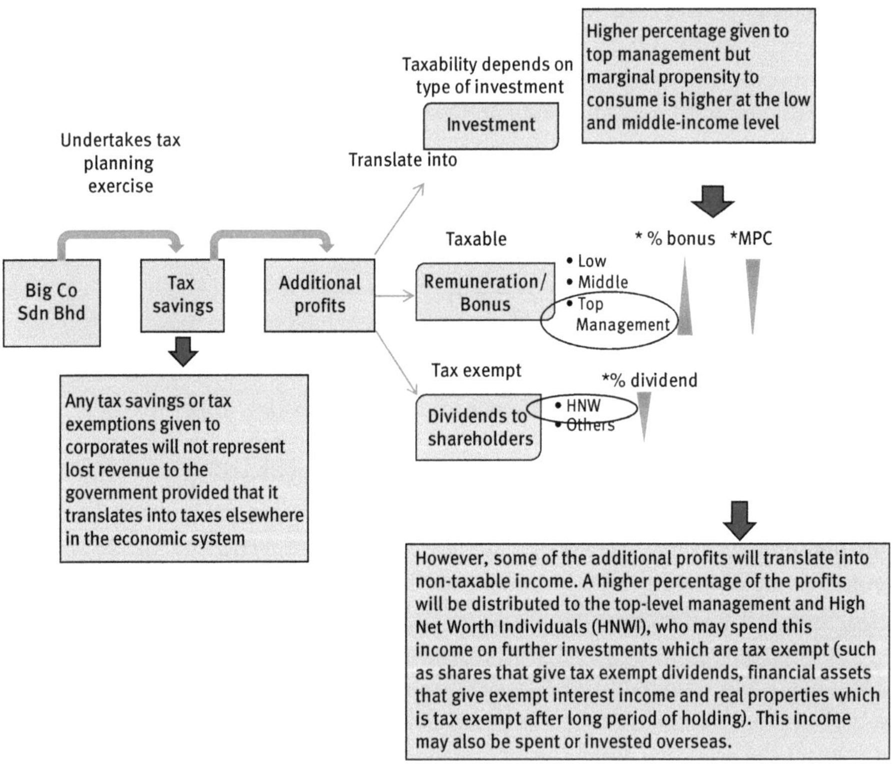

Figure 2.6: Flow of Lost Tax Revenue.

There may not have been enough efforts made to understand and monitor these activities by the IRB. Just as the sophistication of financial structures beyond the comprehension of regulators and authorities have contributed to the losses in the recent financial crisis, increased sophistication of tax structures utilizing the loopholes in existing tax laws can also lead to massive losses to the government. As it stands, there are not many taxpayers who are active contributors. Having those active taxpayers declaring less income than owed would exacerbate the already dire situation.

2.5.2 Real Property Gains Tax

There is no capital gains tax in Malaysia; which means any gains arising from the disposal of capital assets do not attract tax. This is a huge advantage to Malaysian taxpayers as the bulk of the income from investment normally comes from realization of the investments. The exception, however, is in respect of gains on disposal of real property or real property shares,[25] which will attract Real Property Gains Tax (RPGT). Rates of RPGT are reflected in Table 2.9.

Table 2.9: RPGT Rates.

Disposal within three years of acquisition	30%
Disposal between the third and fourth year	20%
Disposal between the fourth and fifth year	15%
Disposal in the sixth year of acquisition	5%

The main purpose of this tax is to discourage speculative trading in properties hence the high tax rate for disposals within three years of purchase. Prior to 2019, resident individuals were not subject to tax for disposal of properties after the fifth year, which means long term property investment is not subject to tax. The rate imposed is considered low, and if the investor is able to hold on to the property for six years, he will avoid paying any RPGT altogether (prior to 2019) or pay a small 5% tax. Normally, investment in properties will give a handsome return. Therefore, the wealthy, who have the capability to invest in properties, are able to profit from the tax system. It is not uncommon for the rich to keep their wealth in the form of financial assets (such as shares) and properties whilst drawing a "just sufficient" salary. As dividend income in Malaysia has been fully tax-exempt since 2014, keeping wealth in the form of shares represents a significant tax advantage for the rich. Unfortunately, many of the poor are unable to enjoy the same advantage. Low and middle-income earners will continue to pay their taxes through hard earned income while the rich earn tax-free income from investment.

25 Real property shares are shares in a Real Property Company ("RPC"). RPC is a controlled company holding real property or shares in other RPC of which the defined value is not less than 75% of the value of the company's total tangible assets.

2.5.3 Sales and Service Tax

Sales and Service Tax ("SST") is a form of consumption or indirect tax. Service tax is levied on certain goods and services such as professional services, medical services, restaurants and hotels at the rate of 6%. Sales tax is a single stage tax charged and levied on locally manufactured taxable goods at the manufacturer level and on imported goods at the point of entry. The rate of sales tax is generally 10%, even though some items such as liquor and cigarettes are taxed at a higher rate. These taxes are paid upon consumption. Sales tax is normally imbedded in the price of goods.

In April 2015, this tax was replaced by a Goods and Services Tax (GST). The implementation of GST, which is a multi-stage consumption tax applied at each stage of purchasing of raw materials to sale of finished goods, is to extend the scope of tax to a wider base. The implementation of GST has been deferred since 2007 to allow for businesses to implement the tax and educate consumers. However, the common perception is that GST is recessionary as it is imposed on everyone regardless of income level. It disadvantages the poor and low-income groups, who have to pay a higher price for most of the items they consume. The same rate of tax applies to all, and GST may be a small price to pay for higher-income individuals, compared to the poor.

GST is meant to be tax neutral to businesses and should not lead to an increase in price of goods. Whatever tax a business has to pay to its supplier (input tax) can be offset against the GST collected from its customers (output tax). Only the consumer is the final bearer of GST. However, if the products sold by the business are exempt from GST, it will not be allowed to claim the input tax attributable to the income on the exempted products. A more detailed explanation of the mechanism, merits and criticism of GST are provided in Appendix A. The government has worked with the affected businesses in implementing a fixed input tax recovery mechanism to offset the costs incurred on the exempted products, but the credit given may not fully cover the potential costs. Additionally, the cost of implementing and reworking the systems within a business organization to cater for GST can be substantial. The question arises on whether these costs are passed on to the consumers, which leads to increase in general price of goods and services. To mitigate this, the government has indicated that the personal tax rates will be reduced once GST is implemented to soften the burden of GST. However, the contrary happened whereby the individual tax rates were increased at the higher tax bracket. However, as the number of taxpayers in Malaysia is small, the benefit of personal tax reduction if any, will not reach everyone who has to pay GST. With about two-thirds of the Malaysian population falling under the low and middle-income group, it is clear that the implementation of GST is going to disadvantage the poor greatly – notwithstanding exemptions from GST that will be given to essential items.

For this very reason, the government that took over the country's administration in the 2018 election abolished the GST in June 2018. The abolishment of GST obviously meant a loss of revenue to the government of approximately RM21billion.[26] With high level of debt servicing, the loss meant the need to recalibrate government's revenue and expenses, including downsizing and prioritizing programmes and projects. As part of the review measures, the SST was brought back in September 2018 to supplement the revenue of the government.

2.5.4 Stamp Duty

Stamp duty is chargeable on certain instruments or documents, such as loan agreements and memorandums of transfer. The rate of tax varies according to the nature of the instruments/documents and transacted values. The many different rates of stamp duties require some knowledge of the Stamp Act and regulations in order to ensure compliance with stamp duty obligations. Similarly, stamp duty has been subject to tax avoidance. The provisions of the Stamp Act 1949 have been used to structure transactions to allow for minimal tax to be paid. The case of under-reporting of value in the documents to be stamped is the most common case of tax avoidance in stamp duty.

2.5.5 Public Sector Borrowing

Public sector borrowing supports government spending when there is a deficiency in government revenue. Hence, it is arguable that debt can be a helpful catalyst to economic growth. However, studies have shown that high levels of debt are detrimental to economic growth (Bezemer, 2012; Cecchetti, Mohanty, & Zampolli, 2011; C. M. Reinhart, Reinhart, & Rogoff, 2012a; C. M. Reinhart & Rogoff, 2010). As debt increases, the borrower's ability to pay becomes progressively more sensitive to drops in income as well as increases in interest rates. At the same time, the probability of default and loss of credit worthiness will increase in the wake of economic shock.

An intrinsic feature of the interest-based system is that the risks of a debt transaction are transferred from the lender to the borrower. The rate of return to the lender is guaranteed, regardless of the outcome of the business undertaking of the borrower. The borrower's contractual obligation to repay the principal together with the interest over a stipulated time frame, notwithstanding his economic situation,

---

26 As quoted by the Ministry of Finance published in The Edge Markets, https://www.theedgemarkets.com/article/rm21b-gst-revenue-loss-be-plugged

in effect disconnects the relationship between the financing and the project for which the funds are needed. The compounding of interest exacerbates the situation resulting in a divergence between the financial and real economy. In other words, a financial system based on debt is not anchored to the real economy. Because of this, such a system may be said to be inherently unstable (Askari, Iqbal, Noureddine, & Mirakhor, 2012).

Additionally, interest-based debt instruments exacerbate income distribution bias towards higher income groups. These instruments are normally sold wholesale and in large denominations such that only the more economically able segment of the population – such as banks and financial institutions, high-net-worth individuals or foreign investors are able to buy them. In the case of foreign creditors, resources are diverted outside the country whilst taxes are levied on the low and middle-income groups to serve these instruments, thus negatively impacting income and wealth distribution.

High debt-interest payments have an opportunity cost. The money paid for debt service may be better utilized in other more productive spending. High government borrowing may also "crowd out" private investment. The term "crowding out" refers to the extent to which an increase in the budget deficit offsets spending in the private sector. An increase in government spending uses financial and other resources that would otherwise be used by private enterprise. An increase in interest rate may also lead to a reduction in private investment and growth. The extent of the "crowding out" effect depends on whether there is considerable excess capacity in the economy, as excess capacity mitigates the "crowding" impact.

It is not uncommon for countries to run budget deficits for years without running into solvency issues. However, high leverage and persistent deficits, as currently experienced by Malaysia, will impair the ability of the policymakers to respond effectively to future shocks. In times of crisis, borrowings will become expensive and limited especially when a country is losing its fiscal credibility and its credit rating is weakening. Debt servicing becomes a burden such that the country may be producing simply to service its growing debt. It may also fall into a "debt trap" where it will need to borrow more to repay its existing debt.

All the above issues point to the need for an alternative source of financing for Malaysia, one that is free from interest-bearing debt. The Malaysian government has long encouraged the participation of the private sector in the development of the nation. In February 1983, the government introduced the "Malaysia Incorporated Concept" as part of its overall strategy to reinforce a new and enhanced relationship between the government and the private sector. It institutionalized the use of public-private sector collaboration towards national development. The Public Private Partnership (PPP) has mainly involved the large corporate sector in Malaysia and has provided the government with alternative means of financing and managing projects.

In order to provide better opportunities to the other segments of the population (non-corporates) to participate in a similar scheme, the partnership project can be extended to the general public at large. By tapping into the individual savings in the economy, the government can avail itself of alternative sources of funds for development projects, instead of borrowing. At the same time, this will help towards the reduction of the budget deficit. Based on the trend of government debt and individual deposits in Figure 2.7, it can be seen that the individual deposits could have financed part of the borrowings taken to fund the government operations and development expenditure up to the year 2016. Had that been the case, the public finance situation of Malaysia could have been more favourable.

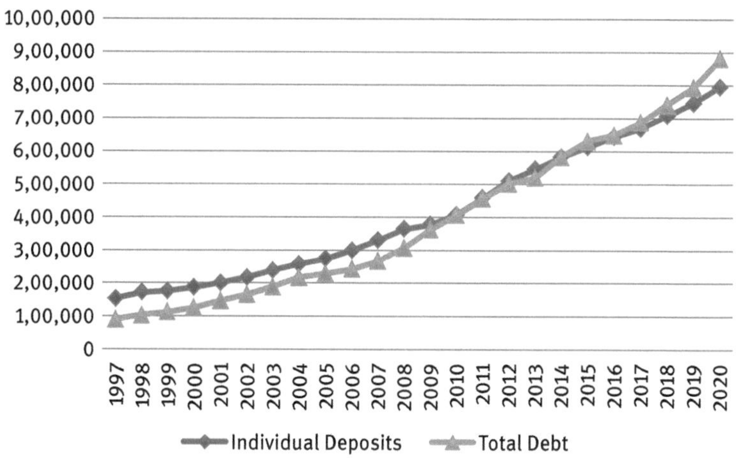

Figure 2.7: Individual Deposits and Debt.
Source: Bank Negara Monthly Statistical Bulletin January 2015 and 2021.

2.6 Conclusion

This chapter has provided an overview of the theoretical foundation of fiscal policy, its tools and current issues relating to the implementation of fiscal adjustments. The point of concern is the effectiveness of fiscal policy in improving economic imbalances and lifting the economy out of a recession or crisis. There are also different schools of thought in terms of how fiscal policy should be implemented – where one favours fiscal austerity whilst another promotes fiscal stimulus. The other area that is closely connected to fiscal sustainability is the level of debt. The use of more debt to solve the existing debt problems seems to only kick the can down the road further towards future disasters. As such, there may be a need to look at an "unconventional" way of addressing the current economic situation from the perspective of the Malaysian fiscal position.

This chapter also discussed in detail the fiscal situation in Malaysia and analysed the taxation policy and the public sector financing policy. Fiscal policy tools currently in use are reviewed, and from the impediments identified, this book will then propose an alternative fiscal structure that may improve fiscal sustainability in Malaysia. This proposed structure is the subject of empirical analysis in the later chapters to determine its viability.

3 Studies on Fiscal Sustainability

3.1 Introduction

The issue of sustainability has normally been addressed in terms of the effects of public debt on the economy – i.e. large budget deficits and increasing ratios of government debt to GDP will generally prompt questions about the credibility and sustainability of fiscal position. The analysis of sustainability involves looking at the components of debts, rates of growth of the economy and interest rates, as well as the expenditure pattern and revenue generated by the economy. It involves some forecasts of government revenue and expenditure, and in some cases, determination of some target ratios of debts and time horizon. Looking at the diversity of assumptions that have to be taken, naturally, there have been many different approaches of assessing fiscal sustainability.

3.2 Fiscal Sustainability

There exists many assessments of fiscal sustainability of a country, such as those by Abdullah, Mustafa, & Dahalan (2012); Aktas & Tiftik (2009); Bogaert (2000); Bohn (2005); Fernandez & Cos (2002); Fredriksen (2000); Krejdl (2006); Marinheiro (2006) and Miners (2000), to name a few. Cross country comparisons were done by Croce & Juan-Ramón (2003), Polito & Wickens (2005) Uctum, Thurston, & Uctum (2006) and Ghosh, Kim, & Mendoza (2013). From these previous studies, it is evident that while the economic intuition indicates that a sustainable fiscal policy must ultimately avoid government bankruptcy, the analytical and operational definition of sustainability is not straightforward. As Balassone & Franco (2000) correctly posited, there is no consensus among economists on a precise operational definition and condition for fiscal sustainability; rather different studies use their own, often similar, definitions and conditions.

3.2.1 Operational Definition

In economic literature, there have been various definitions of fiscal sustainability. The first and oldest specification, dating back to Domar (1944), requires the public debt ratio to converge to a finite value in order to avoid a continuously growing tax ratio. Buiter (1985) defined a sustainable policy as one capable of keeping the ratio of public sector net worth to output at its current level. A similar definition was proposed by Blanchard, et. al (1990), who defined fiscal sustainability as the ratio of debt to GDP that converges back to its initial level. Hence, the concern is whether a

https://doi.org/10.1515/9783110591187-003

government is headed towards excessive debt accumulation. However, the fact that debt does not rise immediately does not signify fiscal sustainability because governments may overspend or finance its deficits using its assets, which will eventually deplete. Conversely, a rising debt does not necessarily suggest an unsustainable fiscal position, as future growth of the economy may be more than adequate to finance the existing debts. Due to these contradictions, Buiter (1985) focused on the country's net worth – which unfortunately is not easy to measure – in assessing fiscal sustainability.

Having said that, defining sustainable policy in terms of convergence of the debt-to GDP ratio or net worth to output ratio towards its initial level is regarded as arbitrary. Firstly, there is no theoretical reason why the debt ratio should be required to return to its initial level and not any other stable level, whether lower or higher. Secondly, it is possible to envision a policy under which the debt ratio rises to excessive levels and later comes down to a "safe" level (Krejdl, 2006).

The above criticisms have been resolved by taking a more general definition of sustainability and by distinguishing between sustainability and solvency, as done by Artis & Marcellino (2000) and IMF (2002).[27] Fiscal sustainability is closely tied to solvency. A sustainable policy is one that, if continued indefinitely and without modification, would keep the government solvent (Tanner, 2013). According to Krejdl (2006), the government is said to be solvent if over an infinite horizon, it is capable of paying its debt via future surpluses. This means the present value of future primary surpluses must exceed the present value of future primary deficits by an amount sufficient to cover the difference between the initial debt stock and the present value of terminal debt stock (Chalk & Hemming, 2000). One commonly used definition in mainstream literature is that to have a sustainable fiscal policy, the government must be able to raise enough resources (in present value terms) to meet its current and future financial obligations without default or major modifications in its current taxation and spending policies. As a prerequisite, a government must satisfy intertemporal solvency or budget constraints (Burnside, 2004; Chalk & Hemming, 2000; Krejdl, 2006; Tanner, 2013). A weak sustainability implies that the government may have future problems in marketing their debt without involving a substantial rise of interest rate that may have perverse effects on economic growth.

In view of the wide range of operational definitions, there are also many approaches used to assess fiscal sustainability.

27 The government is said to be solvent if over an infinite horizon, it is capable of paying its debt via future surpluses (Krejdl, 2006)

3.2.2 Theoretical Framework

The general analytical background for assessing fiscal sustainability focuses on the present value budget constraint as a benchmark for solvency. An overview of the different approaches in assessing fiscal sustainability was done in an International Monetary Fund (IMF) Working Paper by Chalk & Hemming (2000) and in a review of fiscal rules set in the Maastricht Treaty by Balassone & Franco (2000). At the same time, the study of debt dynamics is also an important element in the analysis of fiscal sustainability. Experience during recent crises suggests that contingent liabilities are often an important source of accretion of public debt (IMF, 2003). Since a fiscal policy stance can be thought of as unsustainable if over time, it leads the government away from solvency, a good starting point for assessing fiscal sustainability is therefore to check whether the conditions for government solvency are met (Croce & Juan-Ramón, 2003). As such, most analytical work on fiscal sustainability take as their starting point a representative agent model in which the government must satisfy both an intertemporal budget constraint and also a static budget constraint in every period.

The assessments of fiscal sustainability can be done either using sustainability tests – which involve econometric analysis – or sustainability indicators. Using the standard definition of fiscal sustainability,[28] various sustainability indicators can be constructed. Fiscal sustainability indicators are used to assess how fiscal policy departs from sustainability. These indicators also measure the fiscal adjustment required to bring public finances back to a sustainable track. Sustainability tests on the other hand, aim at verifying whether the solvency condition has held for past budgetary policies and based on these results, try to infer lessons for the future.

These sustainability studies can be grouped into: 1) those that assess whether past policies have been sustainable (backward-looking approach); and 2) those that assess the sustainability of future budget balances (forward-looking approach). The first approach econometrically tests whether the development of fiscal variables in a given period in the past suggests that policies have met the conditions of government budget constraints. Hamilton & Flavin (1986) and Trehan & Walsh (1991) are examples of studies that uses tests of stationarity of public debt and public surplus, as well as government expenditure and revenue to determine whether the fiscal policy is sustainable. A non-stationary result indicates an unsustainable fiscal position. Another method tests the cointegration relationship between different fiscal variables. Afonso (2005) and Marinheiro (2006) tested the cointegration between government revenue and expenditure and checked for the value of the coefficient of expenditure in the cointegration regression with revenue. Other studies such as

28 That is, fiscal policy is said to be sustainable if the present value of future primary surpluses equals the current level of debt.

Bohn (1991, 2005) and Croce & Juan-Ramón (2003) econometrically tested for a positive relationship between primary surplus and initial public debt ratio. Croce & Juan-Ramón (2003) in particular specified a target debt ratio towards which there should be sufficient yearly adjustments in primary balance as an indication of fiscal sustainability. Therefore, rising public debt may be sustainable as long as it is below the target ratio.

These backward-looking approaches have contributed towards much of the literature on fiscal sustainability assessment and provided valuable insights to fiscal policy design in the past. However, a criticism of such an approach is that it does not guarantee that the same policy regime will apply in the future. In studies that involve the use of some target ratios, the targets are also chosen arbitrarily. As such, other studies have taken the forward-looking approach.

In a forward-looking approach, fiscal policy is assessed by analyzing future development of public finances based on currently available information and a number of macroeconomic and demographic assumptions. Such studies were fueled by the growth of the public sector and the unfavorable demographic trends that lean towards substantial prospective increases in public expenditure. For example, as the ageing population of countries increases, so do the liabilities on the welfare system. The additional tax burden required to finance these expenditure increases becomes the primary concern. Therefore, it becomes necessary to estimate the future deficit path implied by the current welfare policies. Krejdl (2006), Langenus (2006) Aaberge, Colombino, & Holmøy (2004) and Gokhale & Raffelhüschen (2000) are examples of studies on fiscal sustainability under a scenario of a future surge in age-related spending. At the same time, literature on fiscal sustainability has expanded to bring uncertainty into the analysis. For example, Barnhill Jr & Kopits (2003) applied a Value-at-Risk analysis to account for the uncertainty faced by the public sector in estimating fiscal risk, and Mendoza & Oviedo (2004)'s fiscal sustainability study emphasizes macroeconomic uncertainty in assessing debt dynamics.

Forward-looking approaches often use projections of government deficits and debt dynamics over a long time period. There normally have to be assumptions on the implicit interest rate on public debt and other budgetary items not directly dependent on the age structure of the population. Hence, a major criticism of such long-term projections is the high degree of uncertainty in the projected items.

Another forward-looking approach is the use of fiscal indicators. Based on long-term projections of deficit-debt dynamics, different synthetic indicators were proposed that try to measure how far fiscal policy departs from sustainability. One of the most widely used indicators are the primary gap and the tax gap as proposed by Blanchard (1990). The primary gap measures the difference between the current period primary surplus and the primary surplus needed to stabilize the debt-to-GDP ratio at a target level (Blanchard, 1990), or the ratio of government net worth to GDP at the present level (Buiter, 1985). The greater the difference, the greater the fiscal effort required to stabilize the debt-to-GDP to the desired level. Tax gap, on the other hand, measures the difference between the current tax rate and the rate of tax that would prevent the debt ratio from rising over the period under consideration. The tax gap can be medium term, covering a period of about three to five years or long term (a period of about 50 years). These gap indicators can be done in an infinite or finite horizon gap. Finite horizon indicators are easier to interpret but completely disregard the developments beyond the given horizon, which may lead to underestimation of the required fiscal correction. The primary gap is useful as it concentrates on the budgetary balance, which is usually the object of policymaker's interest. However, it may substantially underestimate the adjustment needed if a surge in spending is expected. The main shortcomings of these indicators are in the arbitrary nature of the choices required about the time horizon and the target debt to GDP ratio at the end of the period. Closing the gap only leads to a given debt level at the end of the period but does not restrict the debt dynamics thereafter.

Notwithstanding the shortfalls, the indicators are useful in that they are quite simple and have a ready method that is easy to interpret. They have also been applied widely. A variant of the tax gap indicator, the S1,[29] has been used by the European Commission in the calculation of sustainability gaps of its member countries.

Other forward-looking approaches are studies that focus on intertemporal fiscal burden for different generations; such as that done by Auerbach, Kotlikoff, & Leibfritz, (1998). The main value add of generational accounting studies compared to the long-term projections and the synthetic indicators discussed above is that they not only signal sustainability problems but also clearly show their potential implications in terms of intergenerational fairness. They can be used to assess the impact of alternative policy responses on the welfare of different generations. However, full-fledged generational accounting exercises tend to be very data-intensive and require an even more important number of assumptions than the synthetic indicators.

3.2.3 Merits and Criticism

Based on the above discussion, the methods which have been proposed for evaluating fiscal sustainability has their appeals and limitations. First and foremost, a common problem with analysing sustainability is that it is based on a partial equilibrium framework, disregarding the interactions between the budgetary policies and the economic environment. Public revenue, expenditure, deficit and debt have an impact on other macroeconomic variables, of which the interest rate and the growth rate of GDP

29 The European Commission typically uses two quantitative indicators in its assessment of the sustainability of public finances in EU Member States. The so-called S1 indicator is inspired by both the tax-gap indicator proposed by Blanchard et al. and the reference value for public debt defined in the Treaty on the European Community. It is defined in the Treaty as the difference between the primary balances required in a certain target year to bring the debt ratio to 60% in 2050.

that lower net inequality is robustly correlated with faster and more durable growth. To balance simplicity, efficiency, fairness and revenue sufficiency, a good tax policy should be easy to implement and administer, will induce social solidarity and increase tax compliance, and not be burdensome to taxpayers. More importantly, it is able to generate the required revenue to the government. Although inequality will always exist within even the most efficient markets, the goal of taxation is to eliminate as much inefficiency as possible.

A good tax system is relevant in the analysis of fiscal sustainability as the revenue generated by a good tax system is able to sustain government spending and borrowing. There are four types of tax system – the proportional or flat tax system where the average tax rate is the same no matter how much a person earns; the progressive tax system where the average tax rate increases as income increases; the regressive tax system, which is the reverse of the progressive tax system and the lump sum tax where everyone pays the same amount of total tax no matter how much income is generated. The third and fourth tax system can be deemed unfair as it is advantageous to the rich at the expense of the poor. The comparison between which is the more preferable tax system has normally been focused on the progressive and flat tax system.

3.3.1 The Case for a Flat Rate Income Tax System

The US and many other countries implement a progressive tax system due to the nature of income inequality that usually happens in a capitalist system. A progressive tax system works on the premise that the rich should bear a higher burden of tax liability to redistribute wealth and prevent a wide income gap. However, the effectiveness of the progressive tax system in achieving the redistribution goal depends on the demographic and legislative environment in which it is implemented. Chapter 2 has illustrated in detail the situations in which the progressive tax system benefits higher income groups such that the supposed effects of the system may not be fully achieved. Progressive tax is also said to disincentivize people in the higher marginal tax bracket from working, as each additional amount earned will increase their taxable amount. As the marginal benefit of extra work falls, people are less motivated to be more productive and creative. A study by Røed & Strøm, (2002) found that the effect of progressive taxation on labor efficiency depends on the elasticity of labor supply and the competitiveness of the labor market. However, results of studies on the effectiveness of the progressive tax system in reducing inequality and improving growth have been mixed. Studies by Arnold (2008) and Duncan & Peter (2008) have shown that there is a negative relationship between progressivity of tax and inequality, albeit very minimal. The minimal relationship could partly be explained by the findings in Chapter 2 where the distributive effect of the progressive tax system is tapered by the presence of tax reliefs and exemptions that opens tax-planning opportunities. Studies by Duncan & Peter (2008) and Duncan & Peter (2012), using a panel of countries, also showed that under certain conditions, tax progressivity may increase actual inequality, especially in countries with weak law and order and a large informal non-taxable sector. However, a study by Diamond & Saez (2011) concluded that the top bracket earners should be subject to rising and high marginal tax rates, and Angyridis (2013) showed that increasing tax progressivity has a profound effect in reducing inequality and a mild negative effect on growth. A study by Angyridis (2013) on the US, as noted by Duncan & Peter (2008) showed the positive effects of reducing tax progressivity (i.e. moving to a flatter tax regime) – via direct compliance response and pro-poor redistribution of increased tax revenues from higher levels of compliance. It is less apparent in developed countries which have a high tax compliance rate to start with. Therefore, it seems to suggest that progressive tax rates may work better in an economy where there is high tax enforcement and low informal economy.

A progressive tax system is also complex, with numerous tax exemptions, tax credits and double tax on certain income. The complexity presents an opportunity for tax leakage through tax evasions and creative tax planning. A study by Slemrod & Yitzhaki (2002) showed that changes in the tax structure tend to lead high income taxpayers overcome a change in their consumption basket by giving new instructions on account reporting, change the timing of transactions and effect actions that maintain a status quo.

Equality is achieved in a progressive tax system by distributing income through imposing a higher tax burden on the rich for welfare expenditure on the poor. However, it has also been argued that equality is achieved when everyone is taxed at the same rate. This is a characteristic argument for the flat tax system. Under a flat tax system, there is no distinction between the income classes; therefore, it is said to be a fairer tax system. It incentivizes work effort as whatever the income level, the tax rate remains the same. The flat tax system is simple and hence more cost efficient to comply with and administer. However, Duncan & Peter (2008) showed that generally, there is a tradeoff between efficiency and equality. Voinea & Mihaescu (2009) indeed found that there is an increase in inequality determined by the flat tax in Romania, and Duncan & Peter (2008) concluded that as taxes become more efficient via lower progressivity (or flatter tax rate), income inequality tends to increase. However, they argued that the increased inequality under the flat tax system is not necessarily the case for all countries. While inequality will likely increase following the implementation of a flat tax, actual income inequality may not change and may even improve in countries that suffer high levels of tax evasion. This finding was found by Paulus & Peichl, (2008) in their study of the effects of a flat tax reform in Western Europe. They concluded that generally flat tax improves labor supply incentives but results in higher inequality and polarization. However, Mediterranean countries with welfare state regimes would be likely to benefit from a flat tax reform. The simplicity and the success of the implementation of the flat rate tax system in terms of growth has prompted many debates and proposal for a change of the tax structure from the progressive to the flat tax system.

The most referred to literature on the flat tax system is the flat tax proposed by Robert Hall and Alvin Rabushka in 1983 – later revised in 1995 – which taxes businesses and individuals at the same single rate. Businesses are taxed on total sales less labour costs, cost of capital goods, and purchase of raw materials, while individuals are taxed on the difference between their total labour compensation and a personal allowance. There is no tax on savings, no double taxation on dividends, and interest income is taxed as part of business income, making it a tax on consumption. The tax is simple such that a tax return can be made on a postcard. The presence of a personal allowance for taxpayers indicates that the flat tax system by Hall & Rabushka (2007) is a modified flat tax. Another variation is a true flat tax proposed by Browning & Browning (1985). Their true flat tax is a low and single rate tax on total income without any preferential treatment given to specific sources or uses of income. A true flat tax is thought to harm low and middle-income earners, which is a politically unacceptable consequence. However, their study showed that a flat tax rate will harm lower income households to a much smaller degree than is generally believed or estimated, and may even benefit them over the long run. Based on their findings, transfer programmes are a better way to ensure adequate income for the truly impoverished. If there are any costs involved from the implementation of a true flat tax, the efficiency gains are sizeable enough to offset a large part of these costs. However, the strong perception that a flat tax would substantially shift the tax burden from the highest income groups to low and middle-income taxpayers – many of whom currently pay little or no income tax – accounts for the reason why current flat tax proposals are actually modified flat tax proposals. These modified flat taxes usually include some variations, such as an income level beneath which no taxes are paid, a small number of allowable deductions, or different rules or rates for business income. Some flat tax plans also have a small number of tax brackets. Technically, this makes them progressive tax plans, although they are far "flatter" than the progressive tax system.

Studies have shown that the implementation of a simpler tax structure such as the flat tax system has the ability to generate more revenue. This was demonstrated in a study by Ivanova, Keen, & Klemm (2005) and Gorodnichenko, Martinez-Vazquez, & Peter (2008) on the 2001 flat tax reform in Russia.[31] However, the effects of the flat tax system in reducing tax evasion or labor informality has been mixed. Mara & Narazani (2011) concluded that the flat tax system has not contributed in the reduction in labor informality in Albania; while Gorodnichenko et al.

31 Its GDP grew at an average compounded rate of 26% over the years 2000 to 2008. Statistics cited in the article, The Rise of Flat Tax Gives Us Morning in Albania, http://www.forbes.com/sites/nathanlewis/2011/09/29/the-rise-of-the-flat-tax-gives-us-morning-in-albania/

(2008) found a large and significant change in tax evasion arising from increased voluntary tax compliance in Russia. There is also a strong evidence of positive relationship between lower tax rate and lower tax evasion.

Latvia, Lithuania and Estonia are countries that have first introduced flat tax in the 1990s. Hong Kong adopted the flat tax idea in 1947 and recently revived it in the 1980s. The success of the flat tax regime has prompted other countries such as Russia and other transitional countries such as Slovakia, Romania, Georgia and Albania to follow suit. Flat tax has become increasingly popular in Eastern Europe, but other countries such as Western Europe, the US, the United Kingdom and Australia with a well-established middle class have only given the flat tax reform a deliberation. Empirical studies have also been done on the viability of change to the flat tax system on countries that have not yet implemented the flat tax system. For example, Labeaga, Oliver, & Spadaro (2008) did a study on the current tax reform in Spain and found potential benefit in adopting a basic income flat tax scheme as a distributional mechanism that can both reduce inequality and increase social welfare. Aaberge, Colombino, & Strøm (2000) studied the labor supply responses and welfare effects of a flat tax reform in Italy, Norway and Sweden and found that flat tax benefits Norway. Caminada & Goudswaard (2010) concluded that from distributional point of view, the idea of a flat tax system could be taken seriously in debates on tax reform in Netherlands. Grecu (2009) suggested that British taxpayers should be allowed to choose between the graduated three-bracket tax system (with all its reliefs and deductions), and a simple flat tax (with a generous personal allowance, but with no deductions) due to the advantages of the latter.

From the discourse above, both the progressive and flat tax system have their pros and cons. While a progressive tax system is more effective in terms of redistribution of income, the flat tax system improves tax compliance and labour incentives through its simplicity. As Malaysia is currently under a progressive tax system and the impediments of the current tax system has been discussed in Chapter 2, there may be some benefits to be gained from the simple flat tax system. As Palil & Mustapha (2011) found, one of the determinants of tax non-compliance in Malaysia is the level of tax knowledge. Therefore, the tax system should also be simplified and made easy to understand.

There have been some studies done on the determinants of tax non-compliance in Malaysia such as those done by Palil & Mustapha (2011); Tabandeh, Jusoh, Nor, & Zaidi (2012) but little has been studied about the progressivity of tax rates and the extent of tax evasion in Malaysia, apart from a mention in a paper by Chen (2012). However, various other studies elsewhere have been done on the relationships between the marginal tax rates and the incidence of tax evasion, such as that by Allingham & Sandmo (1972); Clotfelter (1983); Feinstein (1991); Gahramanov (2009); Laszlo (2003). The study by Allingham & Sandmo (1972) showed that tax evasion tends to increase with marginal tax rates. Clotfelter (1983) has found that the elasticity of underreported income with respect to marginal tax rates is positive, which suggests that tax evasion will increase with an increase in the marginal tax rate. Therefore, any consideration for a tax reform should include a reduction in the marginal tax rate to lower the tendency for tax evasion.

It is widely acknowledged that Malaysia needs to widen its tax base. The move taken by the government in 2015 to introduce GST raised many concerns about reduction in purchasing power among the population. This was further confirmed in a study by Palil & Ibrahim (2011). Their study also suggested that there would be a significant change in consumption behaviour; i.e. people will be more prudent and selective in their purchasing behaviour, which would potentially distort aggregate demand. Proponents of GST argue that the generation of information on transaction chains in such a tax system is useful for enhancing the probability of detection of informal activities. However, because of the "tax interaction effects" between income tax and GST, the well-meaning presence of special provisions and exemptions in most GST and income tax systems put in place to protect the interests of the poor or special interest groups increases the incentive to cheat (Ahmad, Best, & Pöschl, 2012).[32]

As Malaysia is currently under a progressive tax system, this book will research the effectiveness of a change to a flat tax structure on the fiscal position. The proposed flat tax structure will include an exemption level similar to the Hall-Rabushka (1995) flat tax to cater for the lower income group, which may already be paying a low tax rate to start with. This minimum level of income is similar to the concept of *nisab* in Islamic alms, *zakat* and one, which could enable a person to live a decent life under current standards of living. The policy reforms being considered will not only look at a simpler tax structure – to reduce the complexity of the current tax system, increase compliance and plug loopholes currently available – but also levy the tax based on the ability to pay such as wealth tax.

3.3.2 A Case for Wealth Tax

> *It is not very unreasonable that the rich should contribute to the public expense, not only in proportion to their revenue but something more than in that proportion*[33] – *Adam Smith*

A wealth tax is a tax based on the market value of assets owned. These assets include, but are not limited to, cash, bank deposits, shares, fixed assets, private cars, assessed value of real property, pension plans, money funds, owner-occupied housing and trusts. Taxing wealth and the wealthy is an important component of social

---

32 For more detailed work on presence of informality in developing countries, please refer to Ahmad et al., (2012) and Ahmad & Best, (2012).

33 *An Inquiry into the Nature and Causes of the Wealth of Nations*, Volume 2, Book V, Chapter II, Part II, Article I (Adam Smith, 1776)

solidarity. As mentioned earlier, the wealthiest 20% of Malaysians control nearly 50% of wealth, while the poorest 40% of the population controls just about 20% of wealth. Malaysia does not tax capital gains except gains on real property. As such, much of the wealth generated through capital returns is tax-free. The ability to generate wealth is only accessible to the rich who have the extra financial capacity to invest in capital investments. As such, taxing wealth may potentially reduce the wealth gap. A study done by Khalid (2011) on the composition and inequality of household wealth in Malaysia showed that the distribution of wealth is more skewed than income distribution. The study found that real estate assets make up about 96% of wealth – of which the top bracket of tax on the gains is only 15% (prior to 2019), while financial assets make up the rest – of which gains are not taxable.

The Muslims in Malaysia pay *zakat*, which is a wealth tax in Islam. *Zakat* is levied on the traditional definition of wealth such as gold, silver, livestock and agricultural produce, as well as other forms of wealth based on the consensus of Islamic scholars and jurists. In Malaysia, employment and business income, savings (including savings in the Employees Provident Fund), as well as financial assets are all subject to *zakat*. The wealth tax proposed in this study is a tax on the total financial assets (including savings and investments) and physical assets (real properties and fixed assets) net of liabilities (further explained in Section 4.5.2). It may be argued that the imposition of wealth tax in this study may result in some wealth of Muslims being taxed twice, such as their savings and financial assets and other wealth, insomuch that the wealth falls within the definition of fixed assets in this study. Under the current income tax regime, a similar double tax is present for employment and business income. This has been mitigated by a rebate given in part or for all of the *zakat* paid against the income tax liability of the Muslim. A similar relief mechanism can be applied to the wealth tax proposed in this study.

Several authors have studied capital taxes or taxes on wealth – such as Atkinson (1971), Hansson (2002), Mcdonnell (2013), to name a few. Boadway, Chamberlain, & Emmerson (2010) have questioned the rationale for a wealth tax on the grounds that it constitutes double or triple taxation i.e. taxation under income tax when it is created, and then taxation subsequently in its own right. However, double taxation is not peculiar to wealth taxes as householders also pay their consumption taxes out of their post-tax income. Mcdonnell (2013) put forward six arguments in favor of wealth tax. The potential revenue yield is one obvious benefit to the government. The redistribution of wealth is often considered the fundamental objective of a wealth tax and it is these social justice concerns which make up the second set of arguments in favor of wealth taxes. Wealth taxes reduce inequality in the distribution of wealth by constraining the accumulation of wealth by the wealthy. Underlying these social justice concerns are the concepts of vertical equity and the ability to pay. Horizontal equity is another benefit. The idea is that persons or groups with the same taxable capacity, or ability to pay, should be treated equally and should pay the same amount of tax. Administrative efficiency and the fight against tax evasion form the basis of the fourth and fifth set of arguments often used to justify annual wealth taxes. Data from wealth tax can be cross-checked against other tax returns to help detect and discourage evasion of other types of taxes. Lastly, net wealth taxes may encourage more productive use of assets by imposing charges on wealth irrespective of income. Because wealth will generally present a much larger tax base than income, tax rates can be kept very low and still accrue substantial revenue.

Even though many popular contentions seem to posit that wealth tax causes capital flight, its effect may not be as alarming as the perception would suggest (Hansson, 2002). A carefully implemented wealth tax on selected classes of assets has the incentive structure that allocates idle assets to productive use by switching from low-yielding investments to high-yielding ones, in order to offset the additional taxes. Most importantly, taxation based on ability to pay is a fairer tax system. Taxes are currently levied on wealth in countries such as India, the Netherlands and Norway. The global financial crisis has caused some countries such as Iceland, Spain, France and Cyprus to re-introduce annual wealth taxes on individuals, some on a temporary basis to alleviate budget constraints.

The bestselling book on the wealth gap by Thomas Piketty, *Capital in the Twenty-First Century*, has once captured global interest. Piketty (2014) analysed a unique collection of data from twenty countries ranging as far back as the eighteenth century, to uncover the main driver of inequality. He demonstrated that in rich countries which are at the frontier of technology and skills, the growth of income is between 1% and 2% a year, while the rate of return on capital averages at about 4% to 5% a year. Therefore, those who draw their income from capital returns will outstrip wage earners, and "inherited wealth grows faster than output and income." He contended that the only way that this can be remedied is with intervention from governments. Otherwise, wealth will concentrate at levels incompatible with democracy, let alone social justice. Capitalism, he concluded, automatically creates levels of inequality that are unsustainable. Therefore, Piketty (2014) proposes a high tax on the top earners and a global wealth tax.

The implementation of wealth tax has not been without objections. Ebb (2004) cited that the fall in fashion of the wealth tax in Europe is due to its contribution on capital drain, high management costs and distortions in resource allocation due to double taxation. Shakow & Shuldiner (1999) noted two administrative weaknesses to wealth tax; one is the need to value assets and liabilities to determine net worth and the other is the need to distinguish between the return on capital and return from labour. Evans (2013) also agreed that valuation is one of the problems in implementation of wealth tax and disclosure being the other problem. There are different categories of assets that would naturally require different valuation method. Assets that are not publicly traded can be very difficult and expensive to value. Even when professional appraisers are involved, there may be a disparity in values especially from the perspectives of the taxpayers and tax authorities that may end up with legal disputes. Therefore, the cost of preparing annual wealth returns may be costly and onerous. The problem of disclosure is that it is very easy to hide many forms of wealth whether in the form of physical assets like diamonds or fungible assets like bank balances. Wealth can be hidden in tax havens. Hence, inequities begin to arise between honest and dishonest taxpayers. Another problem with wealth tax is liquidity. Assets are normally held in an illiquid form. When a wealth tax is imposed on these assets, the taxpayer would need to dispense of the entire property in order to obtain the fund necessary to pay the tax.

Implementation of any new tax will normally be met with criticism. However, on the basis that the tax net has to be widened and to balance the inequality created by the flat tax system suggested by empirical studies, the tax reform proposed in this book will include a flat tax on wealth. The possession of wealth, especially by the rich adds to the capacity to pay tax. Therefore, in the interest of equity, it is justifiable to tax wealth in addition to income.

3.4 Public Sector Borrowing

Another component fundamental in a fiscal sustainability study is government debt. Borrowings supplement any shortfall in government revenue and as such assist in the continuation of economic development. According to the conventional view of public debt, in the short run, output is demand-determined, and fiscal deficits (or higher public debts) have a positive effect on disposable income, aggregate demand, and overall output (Elmendorf & Mankiw, 1999). The recent global recession and the European sovereign debt crisis have stirred an intense debate about the effectiveness of fiscal policy and the consequences of rising government debt. Some economists and commentators suggest that this is the right time to apply expansionary fiscal policy (DeLong & Summers, 2012; Krugman, 2011). Other economists have argued that high levels of public debt have a negative effect on economic growth (Baum, Checherita-Westphal, & Rother, 2013; Cecchetti et al., 2011; C. M. Reinhart & Rogoff, 2009, 2010).

Concern about high levels of debt and its effect on fiscal sustainability centers on whether the growth of the economy is large enough to support the interest on the debts taken. However, the money used to service the debts represent opportunity lost for potential development projects that are necessary to grow the economy. Therefore, the next question is how far does debt affect growth?

3.4.1 Debt and Growth

The framework on the effect of growing debt on interest rates and growth was used by Domar (1944). The main concern was whether "continuous government borrowing results in an ever-rising public debt, the servicing of which will require higher and higher taxes" (p.148). Domar argued that the problem of the burden of the debt is a problem of achieving a growing national income. According to Domar, attempting to reduce the public debt by cutting government expenditure (thus removing a significant source of income and growth from the economy) is largely self-defeating and exactly the wrong course of action when the economy is struggling. The other end of the spectrum is the view that governments should engage in fiscal austerity in times of economic downturn, as debt is not good for growth.

A study by Reinhart & Rogoff (2010) found a close correlation between high levels of public debt and slow economic growth. It suggests that a debt to GDP ratio of more than 90% will stifle growth. However, the findings of subsequent researchers (Herndon, Ash, & Pollin, 2014) on a technical error in Reinhart & Rogoff's work sparked a serious debate on the debt-growth relationship. They (Herndon et al., 2014) found that high debt is correlated with somewhat lower growth, but the relationship is much more tenuous and there are lots of exceptions to the rule. Nevertheless, Reinhart & Rogoff defended their findings in 2010 which are consistent with the findings in their later work on debt overhang (C. M. Reinhart, Reinhart, & Rogoff, 2012b). Supporters of austerity measures have clung to the notion that while the 90% debt-to-GDP threshold in the Reinhart-Rogoff study was inaccurate, its conclusion that high debt slows economic growth remained relevant. Arcand, Berkes, & Panizza, (2012) showed that there is indeed a case of "too much finance". Their study suggested that finance starts having a negative effect on output growth when credit to the private sector reaches 100% of GDP.

Pescatori, Sandri, & Simon (2014) however, found no evidence of any particular debt threshold above which medium-term growth prospects are dramatically compromised, but instead found that debt trajectory can be as important as the debt level in understanding future growth prospects, since countries with high but declining debt appear to grow equally as fast as countries with lower debt. They also found some evidence that higher debt is associated with a higher degree of output volatility and volatile growth can still be damaging to economic welfare. Therefore, concern about the effect of debt on the economy remains valid.

3.4.2 Interest-Based Borrowing

> *What can be added to the happiness of a man who is in health, out of debt, and has a clear conscience?*[34]
> – *Adam Smith*

The financial crisis and its aftermath have demonstrated that this view may be extended to countries as well. There are many justifications which economists can make for the payments of interest, and for many years the interest-based financial system has worked well and brought economic development as can be seen today. However, the real test is to study the effects that interest has on the quality of development. Interest is payment for the use of money, but money in its original purpose is not a commodity. This characteristic of interest has led to some disturbing consequences. For example, interest is the creation of more money out of the initial money without any increase in real tangible assets.

Firstly, interest leads to an inequitable distribution of income. An intrinsic feature of interest is that the risks of a debt transaction are transferred from the financier to the borrower. Therefore, those who borrow become poorer and the rich with the means to lend money become richer. The borrowers promise to repay the principal, together with the interest over a stipulated time frame, notwithstanding his economic situation. This in effect cuts off the relationship between the project for which the funds are needed and its financing. Over time, this process leads to the rapid growth of the financial sector compared to the real sector of the economy. The financial sector, whose original purpose was to serve the real sector, takes on a life of its own and gradually decouples from the real sector. This creates a phenomenon known as "financialization", resulting in a divergence between the real sector and the financial sector of the economy (Askari, et. Al., 2012; Mirakhor, 2010; Othman & Mirakhor, 2013). This phenomenon renders the economic system unstable, as the liability of the economy becomes a large multiple of the assets available to validate them (Mirakhor, 2011).

Secondly, interest widens the gap between the rich and the poor as the distribution of income becomes more skewed over time. When interest payment in interest-based borrowing is compounded, those that are in debt pay interest that grows every year, which further exacerbates the skewed distribution of income. A study by Ranciere & Kumhof (2010) found that high leverage and crises can arise as a result of changes in the income distribution. They found a large increase in the income share of the rich and their bargaining power, as well as a large increase in debt leverage among poor and middle-income households. This was a result of recycling part of the additional income gained by high income households back to the rest of the population by way of loans, thus increasing the probability of a major crisis. According to Rajan, (2010), the roots of the crisis lay in several structural economic

34 *The Theory of Moral Sentiments*, Part 1 Section III Chapter 1.7 (Adam Smith, 2010), p. 34–37

fractures that existed long before the crisis erupted, but were either not properly dealt with or were intentionally ignored. He cited income inequality as one of these fractures.

Thirdly, as the bargaining power of the wealthy increases, production will be geared towards those who have the money to pay for the output, regardless of how necessary other goods may be for society. Fewer resources will be allocated to the needs of the poor, pushing up the price of these goods and further harming the overall economic situation of the poor. They may then be unable to advance socially and economically, leading to a skewed balance of economic power. To the extent that any tax revenues are used to service debt, the burden of debt financing falls on the entire tax base (Salti, 2011). Social crimes and unrest, as well as political instability, may result from widespread poverty.

Therefore, a country may be rich but still possess a debtor society. For example, the economy of Malaysia is growing (albeit slowly in the light of the economic downturn) but the level of household debt is growing at a faster rate. According to the latest Bank Negara Malaysia annual report, household debt to GDP ratio in the country increased by 12.8% within a span of 1 year to 93.3% by end of 2020 from 82.7% at end of 2019. This could have partly been contributed by the economic impact of the Covid-19 pandemic.[35] Prior to that, the household debt to GDP had been experiencing a downward trend from 86.8% in 2013 to 82.7% in 2019. The growth of debt must be managed in order to avoid a debt crisis.

A study by Reinhart & Rogoff (2009) suggested that all crises of the past have been debt crises at their core, regardless of whether they were labeled as "currency" or "banking" crises. It has also been estimated that there are about US$200 trillion worth of paper securities in the global economy, of which US$150 trillion are interest rate-based debt instruments (Rogoff, 2011). Continued transfers of risk with interest rate-based debt instruments do not serve the collective welfare. Risk sharing may well provide an efficient replacement (Mirakhor, 2012).

3.4.3 Risk Sharing System

As opposed to a system where resources and risks are borne by individual operators, a system that pools resources – be it financial, entrepreneurial or technical, will result in greater output and larger profits (Mirakhor, 2010). Additionally, Askari et al. (2012) provided an elaborate justification for risk sharing as a viable alternative foundation for the financial system and how the risk-sharing principle is closely tied to the real sector of the economy. Shiller (2003, 2009) pointed out that risk

35 Bank Negara Malaysia Annual report 2020, accessed from https://www.bnm.gov.my/o/ar2020/index.html

sharing on a large scale can carry with it benefits far beyond that of reducing poverty and diminishing income inequality. He suggested macro market instruments of risk sharing.

Sharing allows risk to be spread and thus lowered for individual participants (Mirakhor, 2012). Risks are shared according to the capability of the bearer. In his study, Fischer (2010) found that equity-like financing, in which partners share both the benefits and risks of more profitable projects, typically overcomes the inefficiencies of partners free riding and overcompensation of peer monitoring, leading to sharp reductions in risk-taking and profitability. The results showed that equity increased risk-taking's expected returns relative to other financial contracts.

Profit and loss sharing and equity participation are the first best instruments of risk sharing (Iqbal & Mirakhor, 2011; Mirakhor, 2010). Mirakhor (1993) analyzed an economy in which there are no interest-bearing assets, only equity shares. He presented an open-economy model to analyze the effects of trade in goods and assets on the macroeconomic equilibrium of the economy. He noted that the absence of interest-bearing assets does not hamper macroeconomic analysis or the workings of the economic system. Instruments of monetary control based on equity with rate of return based on budgetary surplus has also been proposed by Choudhry & Mirakhor, (1997) and Sari & Mirakhor, (2012).

Public policy plays a crucial role in creating an effective incentive structure to promote risk sharing. Therefore, this study will look at a macroeconomic policy framework based on instruments of risk sharing as an alternative to public sector financing.

3.5 Conclusion

This chapter first discussed fiscal sustainability and the various ways of measuring it. The author is of the view that there is no one method that can fully satisfy an assessment of how sustainable the fiscal policy of a country is. Sometimes, the choice depends on the economic circumstances and availability of data on the country. Based on the objective of utilising a fiscal sustainability assessment that is easy to interpret, is widely used, and also to minimise the shortcomings of both the fiscal sustainability indicators and fiscal sustainability tests, this book will assess the fiscal sustainability of Malaysia using both the sustainability indicator and sustainability test.

This chapter proceeded with the discussion of the various literatures that assess the different types of tax structures. In particular, the pros and cons of a flat tax system as opposed to a progressive tax system. As this book is looking at the application of a flat tax system, its application in various countries was evaluated. At the same time, the imposition of wealth tax in various studies was discussed. The author is of the view that there are merits in the flat and wealth tax system that can be applied in the case of Malaysia, to overcome the impediments in the country's current tax system. At the same time, the many discourses on the faults of an interest-based financing system strengthens the view that an interest-free financing system should be considered for public financing in Malaysia. Leveraging on Malaysia's success in implementing Islamic finance, a risk-sharing public financing mechanism will be considered as an alternative fiscal structure for Malaysia. These proposed fiscal structures will be assessed in later chapters in terms of its contribution for fiscal sustainability in Malaysia.

4 Data Description and Modelling

4.1 Introduction

This chapter defines the scope and limitations of the research design, describes the sources and procedures adopted in the collection and extraction of data and the empirical techniques applied to process and analyze the data in order to achieve the research objectives. In addition, this chapter presents the model for the proposed new fiscal policy regime for Malaysia.

The aim of this study is not only to determine the fiscal sustainability of Malaysia under an actual scenario, but also to assess the sustainability under a simulated fiscal policy regime that is designed to include features of risk sharing financing and a flat tax system. At this juncture, it is important to emphasize that the basis of this study is simply an accounting remodeling of the Malaysian national income accounts based on a flat tax structure and an interest-free government financing in order to arrive at a simulated data to compare two different fiscal regimes. It utilizes a simple accounting operation to simulate data of the government budget to remodel the current fiscal policy into a new fiscal framework and then utilize statistical and econometric methodology adopted by previous literatures to test the fiscal sustainability of the different fiscal frameworks.

Various sources are used to collect the data to address the research questions and to extrapolate information that is not readily available. Assessment and evaluation are based on results of statistical and econometric procedures and also on intuitive arguments based on historical trends, economic reports and forecasts, as well as from the author's own experience. Apart from modern econometric approaches, diagrammatic and tabular data representations are used to locate the association, correlation and relationship between related variables and results.

4.2 Research Design and Appropriateness

This book entails assessing a hypothetical economic condition where there is no readily available data to test the research questions. Therefore, the research has been designed around a fiscal model that utilizes simulated data of the fiscal variables of interest. This study involves three components: firstly, simulation of the fiscal position under a new policy structure; secondly, assessment of the sustainability of current and proposed fiscal policy using an indicator of fiscal sustainability and fiscal sustainability test; and thirdly, using the same methodology, assessment of the impact of the new policy structure on fiscal sustainability.

In the context of studies in the Islamic economy, theoretical models have been developed by Ul Haque & Mirakhor (1999); Haider (1997); Hassan & Siddiqui (1994);

https://doi.org/10.1515/9783110591187-004

Mirakhor (1993) and Mirakhor & Zaidi (1991); to demonstrate the workings of an economy under an interest-free system. Instead of calibrated empirical modeling, this study utilizes the time series properties of the fiscal variables of interest in order to assess the existing and proposed fiscal framework. This approach is considered feasible as it uses actual fiscal variables. It entails assessing a hypothetical economic condition where there is no readily available data to test the research questions. Therefore, the research has been designed around a fiscal model that utilizes simulated data of the fiscal variables of interest. The simulated data are derived from data on actual income, expenditure and proxies of wealth, and used as a basis for hypothesis testing using a selected econometric methodology to arrive at a conclusion on the effectiveness or otherwise, of a new fiscal framework.

The empirical testing was conducted on the actual and simulated data to address the fiscal sustainability of the following scenarios:
1. The existing fiscal condition in Malaysia, represented by *R* and *GG*
2. Malaysian fiscal situation with a reformed tax structure based on a flat tax system, represented by *GG* and *NR*
3. Malaysian fiscal situation with a reformed government financing policy based on interest-free financing, represented by *R* and *NGG*
4. A reformed fiscal situation based on a flat rate system and interest-free government financing policy, represented by *NR* and *NGG*

Where *R* and *NR* are the actual and simulated government revenue respectively, *G* is government expenditure (excluding interest payment), *GG* and *NGG* are the actual and simulated government expenditure including interest payment ($G_t + r_t D_{t-1}$) respectively, *r* is the real interest rate and *D* is government debts.

The flat tax system is a tax structure that comprises flat rate tax on income and wealth only. The interest-free financing refers to financing through issuance of Equity Participation Shares (EPS) to the general public at low denominations.[36]

Thereafter, the study will assess the merit of the fiscal sustainability under the reformed fiscal framework (scenario 4) against the existing fiscal framework (scenario 1).

4.3 Model Specifications

This study of fiscal sustainability is based on the commonly used definition of fiscal sustainability in mainstream literature; that is, to have a sustainable fiscal policy,

36 An elaboration of the features and rationale for the proposed tax structure and EPS are given in the next two chapters.

the government must be able to raise enough revenue (in present value terms) to meet its current and future financial obligations without default or major modifications in its current taxation and spending policies. The general analytical background for assessing fiscal sustainability focuses on the present value budget constraint as a benchmark for solvency.

The assessment of fiscal sustainability can be done either by using sustainability tests – which involve econometric analysis – or sustainability indicators. Fiscal sustainability indicators are used to assess how fiscal policy departs from sustainability. Sustainability tests on the other hand, aim at verifying solvency condition for past budgetary policies and based on these results, attempt to infer lessons for the future. Two empirical frameworks have been used to test for fiscal sustainability. The first framework rests mainly on testing the stationarity of the various fiscal variables, where non-stationarity implies an unsustainable fiscal position. Studies by Arestis, Cipollini, & Fattouh (2004); Bajo-Rubio, Díaz-Roldán, & Esteve (2004); Sarno (2001) Makrydakis, Tzavalis, & Balfoussias (1999) and Hamilton & Flavin (1986) are among those that used this approach of testing unit root of fiscal variables. The second employs cointegration time series techniques and explores the existence of a long-run equilibrium relationship between the fiscal variables of interest. This methodology was adopted in studies done by Escario, Gadea, & Sabaté (2012); Bajo-Rubio, Díaz-Roldán, & Esteve (2010); Baharumshah & Lau (2007); Arghyrou & Luintel (2007); Goyal, Khundrakpam, & Ray (2004) and Hakkio & Rush (1991). Abdullah, Mustafa, & Dahalan (2012) for example, used VAR and cointegration analysis to study Malaysian fiscal sustainability. The second approach of using sustainability indicators such as those done by Polito & Wickens (2012, 2005); Croce & Juan-Ramón (2003); Buiter, (1985) and Blanchard (1990); assesses the sustainability of fiscal policy using an index that measures the desired level of debt-GDP ratio in period $t+n$ to its forecast or target value.

This study utilizes both the sustainability indicator and the sustainability test to assess the sustainability of the Malaysian fiscal position as both approaches have their advantages and shortfalls. The result of one sustainability assessment can be compared to the other to corroborate the conclusion of the empirical testing.

4.3.1 Fiscal Sustainability Indicator

The use of indicators of the fiscal stance is favoured by official agencies such as the European Commission (European Commission, 2007, 2010) and International Monetary Funds (International Monetary Fund, 2009a, 2009b). The European Commission has recently adopted such fiscal indicators, S1[37] and S2[38] in determining the fiscal ratios of its member countries (European Commission, 2006, 2007). To keep this study focused on the variables of interest in the area of fiscal policy, this study utilizes the fiscal sustainability index similar to Croce & Juan-Ramón (2003) as opposed to that used by Polito & Wickens (2012), which involve the use of monetary variable in the fiscal sustainability index.[39] It econometrically tests for a positive relationship between primary surplus and initial public debt ratio. Croce & Juan-Ramón (2003) in particular specify a target debt ratio towards which there should be sufficient yearly adjustment in primary balance as an indication of fiscal sustainability. Therefore, rising public debt can be sustainable as long as it is below the target ratio. To monitor fiscal sustainability, this study used a recursive algorithm derived from the law of motion of the debt-to-GDP ratio; subject to a government reaction function that links convergence to the targeted debt ratio with primary fiscal surplus. The sustainability indicator generated is similar to that proposed by Blanchard (1990). It has the advantage of generating results using current, past and target values of relevant variables without any estimation of future GDP and interest rates, and easy to interpret. Unlike Blanchard's indicator, it does not require explicit forecast of either primary surplus, real interest rate or rate of growth; instead, it implicitly treats the current values of these variables as if they were to remain constant in the future.

The starting point for an assessment of fiscal sustainability is the government's intertemporal budget constraint (GIBC). The condition for meeting GIBC is briefly explained in section 4.3.3 below. The sustainability indicator is derived from the intertemporal budget constraint of the public sector where the financing requirements of the government (GFR) induces a change in the stock of total debt $(D_t - D_{t-1})$, to finance the primary deficit PD_t and interest payments on public debt $i_t D_{t-1}$. This is represented by the equation below:

---

37 SI is the European Commission's multidimensional approach in assessing fiscal sustainability that integrates the medium-term fiscal challenges, through fiscal gaps related to the excess of projected government expenditure, including projected age-related expenditure, notably on pension, health care and long-term care, over projected revenue together with any gap with respect to the steady adjustment in the structural primary balance until 2020, to bring the debt-to-GDP ratio to 60% of GDP by 2030. Specifically, one component of the S1 indicator corresponds to the gap between the current (or initial) structural primary balance and the debt-stabilising primary surplus to ensure sustainability.

38 S2 is a similar fiscal sustainability assessment to S1 but integrates long-term fiscal challenges, through fiscal gaps related to the excess of projected government expenditure, including projected age-related expenditure, specifically on pension, health care and long-term care, over projected revenue together with any gap with respect to the primary balance needed to ensure that the debt-to-GDP ratio is not on an ever-increasing path.

39 The assessment of fiscal sustainability using index of the fiscal stance based on log linearization of the government budget constraint as in Polito & Wickens, (2012) may be subject of subsequent study.

$$\text{GFR} = (D_t - D_{t-1}) = G_t - R_t + i_t D_{t-1} = PD_t + i_t D_{t-1} \tag{1}$$

where D is the stock of debts, G is government expenditure, R is government revenue and i is interest rate on government debts. A detailed derivation of equations (1) to (8) is given in Appendix C. To keep the equation simple, it is assumed that net privatisation proceeds, seigniorage and revaluation of assets and liabilities are equal to zero. Note that $G_t - R_t$ is the primary deficit (PD_t) when $G_t > R_t$ or primary surplus (PS_t) if $G_t < R_t$. This equation shows that debt will accumulate as the government runs primary deficits. Stating the above in terms of primary surplus, or multiplying equation (1) by –1 (given that $PS_t = -PD_t$) gives the following:

$$PS_t = i_t D_{t-1} - (D_t - D_{t-1}) \tag{2}$$

By rearranging and dividing the above by GDP (Y) and expressing the change of nominal GDP in terms of the growth rate of the real GDP (g) and the inflation rate (π) as $\frac{Y_t}{Y_{t-1}} = (1+\pi_t)(1+g_t)$, the above equation gives the law of motion of the debt-to -GDP ratio or debt ratio, d_t:

$$d_t = \beta_t \ d_{t-1} - ps_t \tag{3}$$

where ps_t represents the ratio of primary surplus to GDP or primary surplus ratio and $\beta_t = \frac{(1+r_t)}{(1+g_t)}$, r_t being the real interest rate and g_t the growth rate of real GDP. In the absence of corrective measures, d_t will increase over time whenever there is persistent primary fiscal deficits and real interest rate higher than the GDP growth rate. Alternatively, d_t can be expressed as $d_t = \frac{1}{\beta_{t+1}} d_{t+1} + \frac{1}{\beta_{t+1}} ps_{t+1}$. Assuming for simplicity that $\beta_{t+i} = \beta$, that is the discount factor stays constant from time t to $t+N$, solving equation (3) forward recursively for N periods will give;

$$d_t = \beta^{-1} ps_{t+1} + \beta^{-2} ps_{t+2} + \ldots + \beta^{-N} ps_{t+N} + \beta^{-N} d_{t+N} \tag{4}$$

From (4), the formal condition for solvency is established, that is, the public sector is solvent when the present discounted value of future primary surpluses is equal to the value of its outstanding stock of debt. This implies a strict condition for solvency where $d_{t+N} = 0$. A relaxation to this strict condition will be for $d_{t+N} = d^*$ where $0 < d^* < d_t$. The above criterion will ensure that the GIBC is satisfied, thus satisfying the necessary condition for fiscal sustainability. However, the above does not give clear policy prescriptions. All the relevant variables are endogenous such that changes in fiscal measures may in turn affect government expenditures, revenues and interest rates whereas the solvency indicators assumes that the projected paths of the primary balance, interest rates, economic growth and inflation are independent. Moreover, the willingness of the government to initiate fiscal consolidation may be affected by shocks in income growth and interest rates. The sustainability indicator as proposed by Croce & Juan-Ramón (2003) tried to overcome these limitations. This algorithm however does not incorporate macroeconomics disequilibria due to its partial equilibrium nature.[40] Nevertheless, it is still a useful indicator of the fiscal position of a country and serves as an easy to interpret monitoring tool.

It is from equation (3) and the following equations (5) and (6) that the law of motion of the debt ratio – equation (7), which includes a policy reaction parameter λ_t, is derived:

$$ps^* = (\beta^* - 1)d^* \tag{5}$$

$$ps_t = ps^* + \lambda_t\ (d_{t-1} - d^*) \tag{6}$$

$$d_t = (\beta_t - \lambda_t)\ d_{t-1} - (\beta^* - \lambda_t - 1)d^* \tag{7}$$

where d_t and d^* are the debt-to-GDP ratio and target debt-to-GDP ratio respectively, β_t is the discount factor and β^* is the target discount factor that would prevail once convergence to the target debt ratio, d^* is attained. Equation (5) simply states the primary surplus ratio and the discount factor that would prevail once there is convergence to the target debt ratio. Equation (6) decomposes the primary surplus into (i) the primary surplus ratio (ps^*) associated with the target debt ratio and (ii) the policy response to the gap between the observed debt ratio and the target debt ratio. λ_t indicates the intensity of the policy response at time t given the debt-ratio gap in the previous period. λ_t is represented by $\frac{ps_t - ps^*}{d_{t-1} - d^*}$ where ps_t is the primary surplus-to-GDP and ps^* is the targeted ratio. ps^* and β^* are the ratios that would prevail once convergence to d^* is achieved.

By substituting equations (3) and (5) into equation (6), the law of motion of the debt ratio is derived:

$$d_t = (\beta_t - \lambda_t)d_{t-1} - (\beta^* - \lambda_t - 1)d^* \tag{8a}$$

Equation (8a) states that if the debt ratio at time *t-1* is higher than the target debt ratio, d_t would converge to d^* if and only if $(\beta_t - \lambda_t) < 1$. The fiscal sustainability indicator (FSI) is $(\beta_t - \lambda_t)$, where:

40 The way to fully address the issue of endogeneity is to specify sustainability within the framework of a general equilibrium model. As explained earlier, this study has opted for an assessment approach that is easy to interpret and at the same time addresses the limitations posed by other fiscal indicators.

$$FSI_t = (\beta_t - \lambda_t) = \left(\frac{1+r_t}{1+g_t} - \frac{ps_t - ps^*}{d_{t-1} - d^*}\right) \tag{8b}$$

If $d_{t-1} > d^*$, d_t would converge to d^* if and only if $|\beta_t - \lambda_t| < 1$. As such, value of FSI_t below 1 indicates a sustainable fiscal position while values consistently above or equal to 1 indicate unsustainability (Croce & Juan-Ramón, 2003).

The above algorithm captures in one integer all the variables for assessing fiscal sustainability that is: real interest rate, growth rate, primary fiscal surplus and current and target levels of public debt. It measures the fiscal stance based on an index that captures variations on the fiscal stance over time and its likely evolution in the short and medium term. The result of this index is analysed for characteristics regarding the trend in fiscal sustainability. To the author's knowledge, previous studies on the fiscal sustainability of Malaysia have thus far been done based on the adoption of unit root test and cointegration approach to test for fiscal sustainability. This study contributes to previous literatures by adopting the sustainability indicator approach to test for Malaysian fiscal sustainability. Time series data from the years 1980 to 2013 are used to compare the fiscal sustainability index under the existing scenario and under the proposed fiscal regime. At the same time, this study proceeds to test the sustainability of the fiscal policy based on similar sustainability tests in Baharumshah & Lau (2007). As compared to previous studies where the sample ends in 2003, the period of analysis of this study is extended to 2013. As shown in Figure 2.2, the debt to GDP ratio continued to rise from 2013 onwards, and save for the year 2019, the year-on-year percentage increase in debt to GDP ratio is higher than the percentage increase in revenue for the same period. As such, extending the data set to the year 2020 will likely produce the same result as that obtained in this current study.

4.3.2 Fiscal Sustainability Test

The budget constraint looks at the long-run relationship between government revenue and expenditure. From the fiscal perspective, maintaining a stable long-term relationship between expenditures and revenues is one of the key requirements for a stable macroeconomic and a sustainable economy. Numerous studies have looked at this relationship such as those done by Neaime (2015); Miyazaki (2014); Hatzinikolaou & Simos (2011); Hakkio & Rush (1991); Trehan & Walsh, (1988) to name a few.

The econometric tests carried out rest on the above two frameworks advanced in the literature, that is stationarity and cointegration tests. Under the first framework, if the deficit series is non-stationary, then it means that it is growing without bounds over time. In other words, subsequent debt will also grow without bounds, rendering fiscal policy unsustainable. In the second framework, cointegration tests were used to explore whether there is a long-run relationship between government revenue and expenses. If such a relationship exists, this means that the respective government is not spending without bounds and is taking into account the revenue it is generating. Subsequently, it will not have to resort to deficit financing to cover its expenses, and debt would be sustainable and will not grow without bounds. Using a similar approach to Neaime (2015) and Miyazaki (2014), this study tests for a cointegrating relationship between government revenue and expenditure to assess the fiscal sustainability of Malaysia.

More specifically, the cointegration test utilises a time series analysis with the Johansen Cointegration and Vector Error-Correction Methodology (VECM) to test the relationship between government revenue and expenditure. A more robust method, the dynamic ordinary least squares (DOLS) that corrects for possible simultaneity bias among the regressors is also adopted. VECM is also used to test for causality between government revenue and expenditure. The purpose is to provide a useful indicator of how policymakers may respond to the imbalances in fiscal position.

The fiscal variables that will be used for the econometric testing are actual government revenue (*R*), actual government expenditure (*GG*), simulated government revenue (*NR*), simulated government expenditure (*NGG*), budget balances *BD* (*R* – *GG*) and *NBD* (*NR* – *NGG*). The following sections outline in detail the process of the econometric tests for sustainability.

4.3.3 Univariate Unit Root Tests

In carrying out the cointegration analysis, the first step is to carry out the unit root tests on the time series properties of the variables under investigation. This is done to avoid problems of estimating spurious relationships. To avoid probable misleading results, OLS estimation cannot be performed until a test to check for unit root is adopted. If a variable is stationary ie it does not have unit root, it is said to be I(0), or in other words integrated to the order of zero. If a variable is not stationary in its level form, then it has unit roots.

This study employed four unit root tests to test for stationarity of the entire series, namely Augmented Dickey-Fuller (ADF) test (Dickey & Fuller, 1981, 1979), GLS-based Dickey-Fuller (DF-GLS) unit root test developed by Elliot, Rothenberg, & Stock (1996), Phillips-Perron test by Phillips & Perron (1988) and the Zivot-Andrews (Z-A) unit root test (Zivot & Andrews, 1992). The Z-A test has the advantage of detecting a unit root in a time series with unknown structural break. The Z-A endogenous structural break test is a sequential test, which utilizes the full sample and uses a dummy variable for each possible break date. The break date is selected where the t-statistic from the ADF test of unit root is at a minimum (most negative). Allowing for the possible presence of the structural break in unit root hypothesis has two advantages. First, it prevents yielding a test result, which is biased towards non-rejection. Second, with the identification of a possible structural break, association of the break on a certain variable with a particular government policy, economic crises, regime shifts, or other factors can be analysed.

Generally, a set of variables are said to be cointegrated if a linear combination of their individual integrated series, which are l(d), is stationary. The ADF and DF-GLS share the same null hypothesis characterized by a unit root. DF-GLS procedure relies on locally demeaning and/or detrending a series prior to implementation of the usual auxiliary ADF regression. DF-GLS test statistics is likely to minimize the danger of erroneous inferences emerging when the series under investigation has a mean and/or linear trend in its data generating process. DF-GLS test is also sufficiently powerful to detect a unit root in small samples (Miyazaki, 2014). The ADF and DF-GLS tests are performed as benchmarks and if they cannot confirm that the variable is I(1), the test is repeated by including structural break in Z-A unit root test. Following standard practice, a constant will be included. To test for unit root, the following regressions are estimated:

$$\Delta X_t = \beta_1 + \beta_2 X_{t-1} + \sum_{i=1}^{k} \delta_i \Delta X_{t-i} + \varepsilon_t \tag{9}$$

where Δ is the first difference operator, X_t represents the fiscal variables of interest (Neaime, 2015). The number of lags, k will be determined by the Akaike Information Criterion (AIC). To determine the order of integration of the series, equation (9) is modified to include second differences on lagged first and k lags of second differences.

$$\Delta^2 X_t = \lambda_1 \Delta X_{t-1} + \sum_{i=1}^{k} \mu_i \Delta^2 X_{t-i} + \varepsilon_{1t} \tag{10}$$

where $\Delta^2 X_t = \Delta X_t + \Delta X_{t-1}$, λ_i, μ_i are constant parameters and ε_{1t} is a stationary stochastic process. The k lagged difference terms are included so that the error terms ε_t and ε_{1t} are serially independent. Equations (9) and (10) are estimated with time trend.

This study will firstly perform unit root tests on the variables *GG*, *R*, *NGG* and *NR* to determine stationarity of the series. It will also perform unit root test on the budget deficit *BD* $(= R - GG)$ and *NBD* $(= NR - NGG)$. The unit root test on budget balance is equivalent to the test of the cointegration relationship among $r_t D_{t-1}$, G_t and R_t. The Z-A test with a single known structural break will be employed to determine the break point in estimating the equation parameters.

4.3.4 Multivariate Cointegration Analysis

According to Hakkio & Rush (1991), if the series of two variables of interest contain a unit root or integrated of order 1, then one must search for a long-run equilibrium relationship between them (Neaime, 2015). Therefore, to check this, the study utilized the efficient maximum likelihood test to test for the existence of a long-run relationship as developed by Johansen (Johansen, 1995). The cointegration analysis proposes that even though two or more non-stationary time series are drifting apart overtime, the series might converge in the long run. The cointegration test used is based on the trace and maximum eigenvalue statistics. The trace test determines r cointegrating vectors' null hypothesis alongside the substitute n cointegrating vectors' hypothesis. If the value of r is 0, then it can be concluded that a long-run relationship does not exist between the non-stationary variables hence no cointegration exists. The Maximum Eigenvalue test determines r cointegrating vectors' null hypothesis alongside alternative hypothesis of (r+1) cointegrating vectors. The Johansen test starts with a vector autoregression (VAR) of the order p represented by:

$$x_t = \mu + A_1 x_{t-1} + \ldots + A_p x_{t-p} + \varepsilon_t \quad (11)$$

where x_t represents (n x 1) integrated variables' vector generally represented as I(1) while ε_t represents an (n x *1*) innovations vector (Neaime, 2015). The two likelihood ratio tests include the trace test and the maximum eigenvalue statistics and are defined in the following equations:

$$J_{Trace} = -S \sum_{t-r+1}^{n} \ln(1-\beta_i) \quad (12)$$

$$J_{Max} = -S \ln(1-\beta_{r+1}) \quad (13)$$

S determines the sample size and β_i gives the ith biggest canonical correlation. In applying this estimation technique to this study, the lower initial lag length is set on all the variables in the unrestricted equation at one period. The lower lag is preferred so as to preserve the degrees of freedom.

The econometric model for this study is derived from the GFR in (1) above. Rewriting the equation for subsequent periods and expressing in debt yields will give the following:

$$D_t = \frac{1}{(1+r)}\left[R_{t+j+1} - G_{t+j+1}\right] + \frac{1}{(1+r)} D_{t+j+1} \quad (14)$$

Solving the equation recursively yields the following intertemporal budget constraint (Miyazaki, 2014).

$$D_t = \sum_{j=0}^{\infty} \frac{1}{(1+r)^{j+1}}\left[R_{t+j+1} - G_{t+j+1}\right] + \lim_{j\to\infty} \frac{1}{(1+r)^{j+1}} D_{t+j+1} \quad (15)$$

By taking conditional expectations, the above can be written as:

$$D_t = \sum_{j=0}^{\infty} \frac{1}{(1+r)^{j+1}} E_t\left[R_{t+j+1} - G_{t+j+1}\right] + \lim_{j\to\infty} \frac{1}{(1+r)^{j+1}} E_t\left[D_{t+j+1}\right] \quad (16)$$

Intertemporal budget balances if and only if the current value of outstanding government debt is equal to the expected present value of future budget balances, that is, the second part of the equation (16) must be equal to zero, as follows.

$$\lim_{j\to\infty} \frac{1}{(1+r)^{j+1}} E_t\left[D_{t+j+1}\right] = 0 \tag{17}$$

The above equation (17) is known as the no-Ponzi game condition. Given equations (1) and (17) and $ZD = D_t - D_{t-1}$, equation (15) can be re-written as follows:

$$G_t - R_t + r_t D_{t-1} = \sum_{j=0}^{\infty} \frac{1}{(1+r)^{j+1}} \left[ZR_{t+j+1} - ZG_{t+j+1}\right] \tag{18}$$

To test whether equation (18) holds, this study checks for the stationarity of $G_t - R_t + r_t D_{t-1}$ after imposing the cointegration vector (1,−1,1). Given that GG_t is defined as current general government disbursements (including interest payments on debts), this study proceeds to test for cointegration in the regression equation:

$$R_t = \alpha + \beta_1 GG_t + \mu_t \tag{19}$$

Estimating equations for and conducting cointegration tests on public expenditures including net interest payments will determine the sustainability of the budget deficit. Researchers such as Quintos, (1995) and Martin, (2000) tested the necessary and sufficient conditions for deficit sustainability by testing whether GG_t and R_t in equation (19) are cointegrated with β=1. However, according to Bohn, (2007) all of the sustainability conditions, be they strong or weak imply that the transversality condition and the intertemporal government budget constraints are satisfied, therefore all cointegrating conditions are merely "sufficient" for transversality. Therefore, to conclude that fiscal policy might not be sustainable when $\beta < 1$ even if there is a cointegration relationship between government revenues and expenditure could be misleading. In line with existing literature, this study will examine the following fiscal sustainability scenario (Baharumshah & Lau, 2007; Martin, 2000; Quintos, 1995):

(a) Strong sustainability condition given by the I(1) process of *R* and *GG* or *NR* and *NGG*, being cointegrated with vector [1,−1] or with $\beta = 1$
(b) Weakly sustainable fiscal position if *R* and *GG* or *NR* and *NGG* are cointegrated with $0 < \beta < 1$
(c) Unsustainable fiscal position if $\beta \leq 0$
(d) The condition of $\beta > 1$ is not consistent with a deficit. It implies that government revenue is growing faster than government expenditure

4.3.5 Dynamic Ordinary Least Squares Estimation

In order to estimate the parameters of the model, the Dynamic Ordinary Least Squares (DOLS) developed by Stock & Watson (1993) with a structural break (break points as given by the earlier Z-A tests) is used. The DOLS estimation of the β gives a more efficient estimate of the coefficient of the cointegration vector than straight OLS. DOLS will handle the possible endogeneity of regressors and small sample bias in estimates. The relevant equation that incorporates dummy variables representing the structural break is as follows:

$$R_t = \alpha + D_f + \beta_1 GG_t + \beta_2 (D_f{}^* \; GG_t) + \sum_{j=-p}^{p} \gamma_j GG_{t-j} + \sum_{j=-p}^{p} \delta_j \; (D_f{}^* \; GG_{t-j}) + \mu_t \qquad (20)$$

where D_f is a dummy variable representing a structural break and j is the number of leads and lags in the DOLS equation and for the initial test, it is assumed the lead and lag length is unity. To check for robustness of the DOLS estimates, the model is re-estimated by increasing the lag length to 3.

Once the equation has been estimated, the Wald procedure is used to test any restriction on the model (Miyazaki, 2014). The Wald test is used to perform tests of hypotheses on parameters that have been estimated by maximum likelihood. The Wald test works by testing the null hypothesis that a set of parameters is equal to some value. In the model being tested here, the null hypothesis is that the two coefficients of interest are simultaneously equal to zero. If the test fails to reject the null hypothesis, this suggests that removing the variables from the model will not substantially harm the fit of that model.

The Wald test is performed with the null hypothesis of $\beta_1 = \beta_2 = D_f = 0$. If the null is rejected then it is confirmed that structural changes took place, both in the intercept and slope parameters.

The above tests are applied on variables *GG* and *R*, *GG* and *NR*, *NGG* and *R*, as well as *NGG* and *NR* to represent scenarios 1 to 4 as stated in Section 4.2 above. The results of the regression equations are then compared.

4.3.6 Testing for Causality

The objective of this section is to inspect the causal relationship between government expenditure and government revenue. The concept of causality is based on the idea that a cause cannot come after its effect. More specifically, variable X is said to cause variable Y, if the current value of Y (y_1) is depending on the past values of X (x_{t-1}, x_{t-2} . . . .. x_{t-n}) and accordingly the history of X is said to be a convincing factor to help predicting Y. According to Granger, (1969), a variable Y is caused by X if

Y is better forecasted from past values of Y and X together rather than from values of Y alone. Four patterns of causality can be distinguished (Baharumshah & Lau, 2007):

a. Unidirectional causation from expenditures to revenues (spend and tax hypothesis). This suggests that the government adjusts revenues to the level of the planned expenditures (Barro, 1979).
b. Unidirectional causation from revenues to expenditures (tax and spend hypothesis). Following this hypothesis, the authorities adjust their expenditures to the level of the revenues so that control over revenues leads to limited growth in the public sector (Friedman, 1978).
c. Bidirectional causality (fiscal synchronization). This hypothesis is based on the equivalence of marginal cost and marginal revenue that the utility-maximising suppliers and demanders of the public services make. In other words, the fiscal authorities made simultaneous decisions on expenditures and revenues. Hence, the two macro-variables mutually reinforce each other. This is the classical view of public finance (Musgrave, 1966).
d. No causality. The authorities can set the level of expenditures and revenues by rule of thumb. This phenomenon reflects the institutional separation of allocation and taxation functions of the government (Hoover & Sheffrin, 1992). This view is also consistent with no cointegration and a sustainability problem.

As mentioned previously, to avoid running a spurious regression (if some of the employed time series have unit roots) and also to check for both long-run, short-run and equilibrium relationship between the variables, a more comprehensive procedure for causality test for variables that are found to be cointegrated is the "Error Correction Model" or "ECM" that was introduced by Engle & Granger (1987). It includes information from the cointegrated properties of time series and allows for causal linkage between two (or more) variables stemming from a cointegrated (or equilibrating) relationship.

If Y_t and X_t are both I(1) and there is a linear combination of Y_t and X_t that is I(0), then Y_t and X_t are cointegrated, and the regression equation is no longer spurious. This provides with the linear combination:

$$\mu_t = Y_t - \alpha_0 - \beta_1 X_t \tag{21}$$

where $\mu_t \sim I(0)$

When Y_t and X_t are cointegrated, an ECM representation could have the following form:

$$\Delta Y_t = \alpha_0 + \sum_{i=1}^{n} \alpha_{1i} \Delta Y_{t-i} + \sum_{i=1}^{n} \alpha_{2i} \Delta X_{t-i} + \alpha_3 \mu_{1t-1} + \epsilon_{1t} \tag{22a}$$

$$\Delta X_t = \beta_0 + \sum_{i=1}^{n} \beta_{1i}\Delta Y_{t-i} + \sum_{i=1}^{n} \beta_{2i}\Delta X_{t-i} + \beta_3\mu_{2t-1} + \epsilon_{2t} \tag{22b}$$

Where equations (22a) and (22b) are bivariate VAR in first difference augmented by the error correction terms μ_{1t-1} and μ_{2t-1}. The test for causality can be done within the ECM formulation (22a) and (22b). X_t does not cause Y_t if all $\alpha_{2i} = 0$ and Y_t does not cause X_t if all $\beta_{1i} = 0$. The test of the coefficients can be done using a Wald test. The change in X and Y is stationary because they are assumed to be I(1) variables and the residual from the levels regression is also stationary by the assumption of the cointegation (Asteriou & Hall, 2007). Among the advantages of ECM is that it is a convenient model that measures the correction from disequilibrium of the previous period. ECM are formulated in terms of the first difference which typically eliminate trends from the variables involved, hence resolving the problem of spurious regressions. It also searches for the most parsimonious ECM model that best fits the given data sets. Most importantly, the disequilibrium error term is a stationary variable, which means the adjustment process prevents the errors in the long-run relationship becoming larger and larger (Asteriou & Hall, 2007).

The causality test gives estimates of the policy maker's reactions to past fiscal imbalances and provides a useful indicator of how the authorities may respond to imbalances in the future. It does not give the sustainability condition, but rather the dynamics of the fiscal adjustment process.

4.4 Simulation of Variable of Interest

This book is about fiscal policy as an element of demand management, separate from monetary policy. The two variables of interest of the study are the two tools of fiscal policy, which are government expenditure and revenue. This study is interested in the effect of a variation in these variables on fiscal sustainability. The policy reform involves two aspects; one is the tax structure while the other is the public sector borrowing policy. Firstly, a simulation will be carried out to generate tax revenue under a new tax structure that comprises a flat rate tax on income and wealth. The tax revenue of the country is simulated using actual data on income and proxy of wealth. A simulation of various combinations of flat tax rates for income and wealth will be made to arrive at the rate of tax that generates the most tax revenue. The selected rate of income and wealth tax will be applied to the data on income and wealth for Malaysia for the period from 1970 to 2013 in order to generate a new tax revenue stream under the new policy structure.

Secondly, for the same period, a simulated data on government expenditure is generated using accounting adjustment of the government's budget to reflect an alternative government-financing framework. Equity participation shares in financing Malaysia's fiscal deficit and development expenditure are replacing the debt. The public finance of Malaysia will be progressively freed of debt service as the debt is reduced.

The data generated from both the simulation exercises are then used in calculating the fiscal sustainability indicator and in assessing sustainability using the fiscal sustainability test. The data for these two variables are simulated as follows:

4.4.1 Simulation of Tax Revenue

Arising from the impediments of the progressive tax systems as discussed in Chapter 2, the proposed fiscal framework is based on a flat tax system on income. Instead of the introduction of consumption tax, which is seen as regressive, it proposes a flat tax on wealth in addition to income to reflect the premise of taxing citizens based on ability to pay. The tax revenue of the country is simulated using actual data on income and proxy of wealth. The income is made up of income of individuals and companies. The wealth is represented by different categories of assets. Derivation of the new tax revenue figure is based on the national income equation:

$$GDP = Y^* = C + I + G + NX \tag{23}$$

where C is private consumption, I is private investment, G is total government expenditure and NX is net exports (exports minus imports). This study has taken NX to be constant. Each component of equation (23) is broken down further below. Given that total private income and investment are made up of income of individuals and firms or companies as well as wealth held by them, and consumption being a function of disposable income, a detailed description of the simulated tax revenue and expenditure is as follows:

$$C = a + b(Y_{DP} + Y_{DC}) \tag{24}$$

$$Y_{DP} + Y_{DC} = [(Y_P + Y_C) - T] \tag{25}$$

$$G = G_{Op} + G_{Dv} \tag{26}$$

where

a = autonomous consumption

b = marginal propensity to consume

Y_{DP} = Disposable income of private individuals

Y_{DC} = Disposable income of companies

Y_P = Private individuals' total income above an exemption level

Y_C = Companies' total income

T = Total tax levied in the economy

G_{Op} = Government operating expenditure including interest on debt

G_{Dv} = Government development expenditure

debts from the years 1971 to 2013. In other words, the increase of an average of 13% in borrowing under the existing regime is no longer required under the proposed fiscal framework. The interest payment from the year 1971 onwards will be correspondingly adjusted by the reduced amount of borrowing. Therefore, the government spending on interest payment will be gradually reduced. The return on investment in the EPS to the investor is tagged to the return on the portfolio of the development project. Therefore, no costs (except issuance cost) accrue to the government out of the issuance of the EPS.

The following equations represent the above:

$$G_t = G_{Dv} + G_{Op} \tag{31}$$

$$EPS = G_{Dv} + (G_{Op} - T) \tag{32}$$

whenever $G_{Op} > T$ and G_{Op} excludes interest payment on debts $(i_t\, D_{t-1})$. Therefore, the new government expenditure is derived as follows:

$$NGG_t = G_t - EPS + i_t\, D_{t-1} \tag{33}$$

The budget deficits will then be:

$$NBD_t = NGG_t - NR_t \tag{34}$$

where N denotes the new budget deficit, government expenditure and revenue. Similar unit root and cointegration analysis are run on the regression equation (19) using the simulated data derived from equations (30) and (33), and the results are compared with the cointegration analysis on the same regression equation that was based on the actual data of budget balance.

4.5 Sources of Data and Variables Used

The study used mainly data from secondary sources. They were sourced from various government and government authorities such as the Central Bank of Malaysia (Bank Negara), Inland Revenue Board, Economic Planning Unit, Department of Statistics and Valuation and Property Services Department's annual reports and technical documents, and the databases of supranational institutions such as the World Bank and International Monetary Fund. The time series data were obtained from various issues of Bank Negara Malaysia's Monthly Statistical Bulletin and Annual Report and World Bank database.

The simulated data were derived from the workings on time series data obtained from the same sources including various issues of Malaysian Annual Property Market Reports and Statistics Year Book of Department of Statistics. The time series covers a period of 43 years from 1970 to 2013. The time series for G_t and R_t are in real terms converted using the GDP deflator. For ease of calculating the simulated data on government revenue and expenditure, annual data have been used. The sources of each data are provided in Appendix B.

4.5.1 Specification of Income

In compiling the information on individual and company income, we attempted to collect data on chargeable income of individuals and companies reported over the years from the Malaysian Inland Revenue Board (IRB). The data on income is required to generate simulated tax revenue based on a flat tax system. However, the IRB's computerized system holds complete data as required by this study only from the year 2004 onwards which is not sufficient for the purpose of this study. Furthermore, as highlighted in Chapter 1, the number of taxpayers compared to the working population is small. As such, the information on income being charged to tax and reported to the IRB may not represent the total income of the population that should be subjected to tax. Therefore, this study has utilized data from the household income survey by the Department of Statistics in order to come up with the data on income of individuals. As the survey was done on an average of three to four years, an extrapolation of the mean monthly household income has been taken for the years in between the survey years. Taking cognizance of the high low-to-middle income earners in the country, this study has set a threshold of pre-taxable income. This is similar to the concept of *nisab*[43] in *zakat*. The threshold is meant to exempt those who earn just enough to maintain a basic life from paying income tax. The Malaysian Income Tax Act, 1967 has also adopted a minimum level of taxable income in determining the banding of progressive tax rates in individual taxation. For year of assessment 2014, an annual chargeable income[44] of RM5,000 (which is approximately RM417 per month) and below are not subjected to income tax. In setting the threshold for this study, there are various benchmarks that have been considered. The most commonly used is the United Nation's absolute poverty line of USD1.25 per day (approximately RM135 per month) at 2005 purchasing power parity. However, it has been argued that the determination of the poverty line income[45]

43 *Nisab* means the minimum amount of property or wealth that must be owned by a Muslim before he/she is obligated for *zakah*. It is also defined as a measurement that determines the obligation for paying *zakah*.

44 Chargeable income is calculated after deduction of tax exemptions, tax reliefs and tax rebates. Therefore, earnings of approximately RM3,000 per month and below will not be subject to tax.

45 The PLI is defined as an income that is necessary to buy a group of foods that would meet the nutritional needs of the members of a household. The income is also to meet other basic necessities such as clothing, rent, fuel and utilities, transport and communications, medical expenses, education and recreation.

(PLI) should make reference to the specific circumstances of the country in question. Ragayah (2010) explained the setbacks of the existing methodology of determining PLI, and in order to improve the accuracy of identifying the poor households, the Economic Planning Unit (EPU) has revised the methodology of calculating the PLI for Malaysia in the Ninth Malaysia Plan 2006–2010. In 2012, the average PLI of Malaysia stood at approximately RM908 per household. Just to note that since then, the Department of Statistics has determined the PLI at RM980 (2016) and the calculation of PLI has been further revised to arrive at the latest PLI figure of RM2,208 in 2019. The government considers a household as comprising an average of 4.4 members. The Malaysia Human Development Report 2013 commissioned by the United Nations Development Programme (UNDP) edited by Salih, Hwok-Aun, & Khalid (2014) instead says poverty is better measured against what households earn in general, rather than by a fixed minimum level. The report measures relative poverty, which sets the threshold at half the national median income. The relative poverty line in 2012 was RM1,813, or half of the household median income of RM3,626. In determining the threshold for this study, consideration has been given to the minimum earnings that are subject to income tax under the existing tax system. For example, given that a chargeable income of below RM5,000 is not subject to tax; with availability of tax reliefs, rebates and exemptions, a person who earns a monthly income of approximately RM3,000 and below per month will not have to pay tax. On the basis that these "borderline" taxpayers should not be made worse off under the new proposed tax structure, the author has made a calculation of the approximate minimum level of monthly earnings that should be exempted from tax. The calculation is based on the respective years' rate of tax, amount of tax reliefs and tax rebates. An assumption has been made that the minimum level of exempted monthly earnings for the years prior to 1994 is the same as that in 1994. Based on the calculation, the exemption level taken for this study is as illustrated in Table 4.1.

Table 4.1: Exemption Level.

YEAR OF ASSESSMENT	EXEMPTION LEVEL (MONTHLY EARNING IN RM)
2012–2013	3,000
2000–2011	2,500
1995–2000	2,000
1970–1994	1,500

Incidentally, the level of exemption above is approximately within the range of the household median income and the relative PLI stated above. Applying the above exemption level to the data of the Malaysian population and the percentage of distribution of households by income class, the percentage of taxable population is obtained. An explanation of how the individual and company taxable income have been arrived at is as per Table 4.2.

Table 4.2: Derivation of Income.

TYPE	DERIVATION OF INCOME	SOURCE
Income – Individual	The taxable income is the mean income applied to the taxable population as derived above. The taxable population has excluded those earning below the exemption level determined above.	Department of Statistics, author's own working
Income – Company	Based on the tax revenue from companies for the years 1970 to 2013, the income of the companies is derived by grossing up the tax revenue using the prevailing tax rates of the respective years to arrive at the chargeable income. This is a conservative figure as the chargeable income (the grossed-up figure) is after applying tax adjustments for non-deductible expenses and tax incentives and exemptions.	Bank Negara Monthly Statistical Bulletins, author's own working

4.5.2 Specification of Wealth

In order to generate data on wealth, we have to first define "wealth". According to the Oxford Advanced Learner's Dictionary, wealth is defined as a large amount of money, property etc. that a person or country owns. Wealth is a measure of the value of all the assets of worth owned by a person, community or country. It is found by taking the total market value of all the physical and intangible assets of an entity and subtracting all debts. Khalid (2011, 2014) in his study on wealth inequality in Malaysia has measured wealth per capita using the sum of total financial assets and real estate holdings. Taking into consideration the definition in these previous literatures, this study has taken wealth to be the total of financial assets (including savings and investments) and physical assets (real properties and fixed assets), net of liabilities (debt obligations such as loans and mortgages). In some cases, proxies have been used to denote the component of wealth. The data on financial and physical assets have been derived from the sources listed in Table 4.3:

Table 4.3: Data on Financial and Physical Assets.

TYPE	DATA/PROXY	SOURCE
Financial Assets		
Shares	Market capitalisation	World Bank Database Note: Data for years prior to 1987 are estimated based on the average rate of growth of market capitalisation from 1987 to 2013.
Savings	Fixed deposits and savings	Department of Statistics, Statistics Yearbook Malaysia various editions
Employee Provident Fund	Total contribution	Department of Statistics, Statistics Yearbook Malaysia various editions
Insurance and Takaful Investment Funds	Life Insurance and Family Takaful Investment Fund (Malaysian Government Papers and Corporate Debt Securities)	Bank Negara Malaysia Monthly Statistical Bulletin various issues
Liabilities	Domestic credit from banks	World Bank Database
Physical Assets		
Real Property	Value of property transactions (residential, commercial, agricultural, industrial and others)	Valuation and Property Services Department annual reports Note: Data for years prior to 1988 are estimated based on the GDP growth for the respective years.
Fixed Assets	Gross fixed capital formation	Department of Statistics

Any data from the World Bank Database, which is in US Dollars, are converted to Ringgit Malaysia based on the exchange rates given in the same database.

4.6 Conclusion

This chapter outlined the design of this research and defined the model that is to be utilized for the purpose of this study. Instead of adopting either one of the two commonly used methods of assessing fiscal sustainability – as done in many previous studies; i.e. either using the sustainability indicator or the sustainability test, this study utilizes both methods in order to explain fiscal sustainability in Malaysia. The methods are applied to two sets of data, firstly the actual budgetary data of Malaysia from the years 1970 to 2013, and secondly on the simulated data of the same variables for the same duration of years. In the interest of simplicity, the simulation method is used instead of theoretical modeling in order to assess a hypothetical fiscal model. The study aims to provide a well-grounded analysis of the performance of fiscal policy under a regime where the taxes are based on a flat tax system, the taxes are based on the ability to pay, and on a public financing policy that is free from interest rate-based instruments. The fiscal policy is also based on the concept of risk sharing between the government and the general public. This chapter further elaborates on the econometric methodology used, that is the fiscal sustainability index and also the test of cointegration with dynamic ordinary least squares method to arrive at the conclusion on the fiscal sustainability of Malaysia.

5 Empirical Analysis

5.1 Introduction

This chapter presents the empirical findings of the study based on the methodology specified in the previous chapter. To summarize, the objective to assess the fiscal sustainability of Malaysia under the current fiscal framework and consider the viability of a proposed fiscal framework to drive Malaysia's fiscal position moving forward. By simulating data based on a proposed fiscal framework, the sustainability of the revised framework is also assessed. The results are then compared to determine the fiscal structure that provides a more sustainable fiscal position for Malaysia.

The results will be presented in the following manner:

1. Fiscal sustainability of the existing fiscal condition will be assessed using the fiscal sustainability index and the same test is applied to the simulated data to determine the sustainability of the proposed fiscal framework.
2. To corroborate the results in (1), the fiscal sustainability tests, that is unit root test will be applied to all the above variables and cointegration test will be done in the following manner:
   (a) Between *R* and *GG*, to test sustainability of existing fiscal condition;
   (b) Between *NR* and *NGG*, to test the sustainability of a proposed fiscal framework based on a flat tax system and an interest-free government financing;
   (c) Between *R* and *NGG*, to test the effect of a proposed interest-free government financing policy on sustainability;
   (d) Between *GG* and *NR*, to test the effect of a proposed tax structure on sustainability.
3. To determine the long-run relationship between the above variables, dynamic OLS will be applied in the same manner as in (2).
4. The results of the DOLS in (3) for *R* and *GG* for the existing fiscal framework and *NR* and *NGG* for the proposed fiscal framework will be compared to address whether the proposed fiscal framework is better for the economy. In addition, a causality test will be applied using error correction model on both *R* and *GG* and *NR* and *NGG* to explain further the relationship between the variables.

The variables *R*, *GG*, *NR* and *NGG* are all stated in real terms. The qualitative analysis of the results obtained is given before the chapter is concluded.

https://doi.org/10.1515/9783110591187-005

5.2 Results of Data Simulation

From the methodology in Chapter 4, the book has created a simulation of a new time series data of government revenue (*NR*) and government expenditure (*NG*), based on the following proposed fiscal framework:

1. A tax system, which is based on a flat tax rate on income and wealth.
2. A public sector financing that is based on the issuance of a risk-sharing instrument to the general public to finance a portfolio of development expenditure undertaken by the government as well as any deficit arising in a particular year.

5.2.1 New Tax Revenue

A simple simulation of tax revenue was done on the time series of income and wealth from the years 1970 to 2013. The objective is to arrive at a viable combination of rate of tax on income and wealth that generates a higher income than the actual tax revenue received during the same period. The stream of tax revenue based on the selected tax rates will be the time series for tax revenue under the new fiscal framework. The range of tax rate selected for income tax is between 15% and 25%; the first being the lowest tax rate among the countries in the Asia Pacific region, and the latter being the prevailing income tax rate in Malaysia in 2013. The rationale for the selection is that the new tax structure should have a tax rate that is no higher than the prevailing tax rate at that time. At the same time, the bottom range of the tax rate should be competitive with the lowest income tax rate in the region (which is the unincorporated business income tax rate for Hong Kong).[46] The range of tax rate for wealth is between 2.5% and 10% – the first being the rate benchmarked against the rate of *zakat* (the Islamic tax on wealth) and the latter being the lowest property tax in the region (which is the general property tax in Singapore[47]). Currently, Malaysia does not impose any tax on wealth except tax on property[48] and the zakat on wealth for Muslims. The results of the simulation of tax revenue under the proposed structure are as shown in Table 5.1.

---

46 Based on the Inland Revenue Department of Hong Kong's website http://www.gov.hk/en/residents/taxes/taxfiling/taxrates/profitsrates.htm

47 Based on the Inland Revenue Authority of Singapore's website https://www.iras.gov.sg/irashome/page04.aspx?id=2094

The 10% tax rate is the general property tax rate in Singapore. The property tax is also applied on owner occupied residential property but at a progressive rate that ranges from 0% to 16% depending on the annual value of the property.

48 The real property gains tax ranges from 5% to 30% depending on the holding period of the property. 5% is only applicable if the property is disposed after six years of being acquired.

Table 5.1 gives a combination of viable tax rates on income and wealth that produces a tax revenue stream that is higher than the actual tax revenue. The viable tax rates (highlighted in grey) are a combination of the possible minimum income and wealth tax rates. Based on the results obtained, a tax rate of 21% for income and 5.5% for wealth are selected as the tax rates under the proposed fiscal structure. The selection is based on the minimum possible combination of income tax and wealth tax rates that produce the highest volume of total simulated tax revenue among the viable combinations of tax rates. The times series of tax revenue obtained using the selected tax rates (after addition of other non-tax revenue) is used in the econometric tests as the new government revenue (*NR*).

Figure 5.1 plots the tax revenue stream (*NR*) under the proposed tax structure against the actual tax revenue (*R*) (data is after adjustment to real terms).

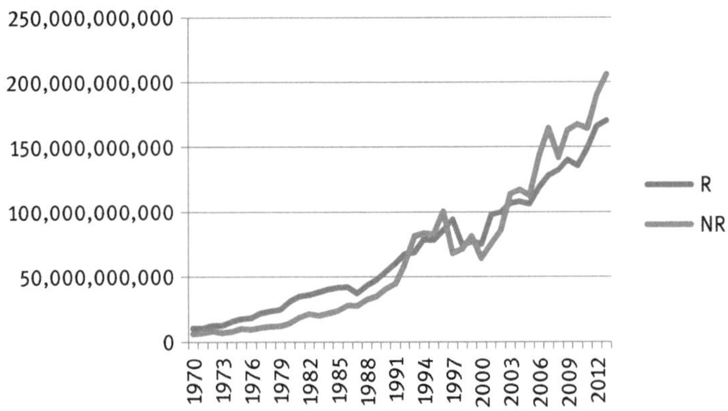

Figure 5.1: Actual Tax Revenue and Simulated Tax Revenue.

The graph shows that *R* and *NR* follows approximately the same trend. *NR* is trailing behind *R* until the year 1993. The proposed tax structure gives higher tax revenue during 1993 to 1997 before *NR* falls below *R*. However, from the year 2003 onwards, *NR* increases at a faster rate than R. The movement can be explained by the structure of the proposed tax system. The component of the tax system is only income and wealth tax. In the earlier years when the GDP of the country is lower, less wealth tax could be collected. The increase in *NR* between the years 1993 to 1997 is consistent with the economic condition in Malaysia during that time whereby the real GDP growth of between 7% to 10% is one of the highest recorded in Malaysian history. The increase of *NR* above *R* continues from 2003 onwards as the economy recovers from the Asian financial crisis, and it is interesting to note that this trend continues during the next period of financial crisis in 2007/2008, even though there is a dip in tax revenue in 2008.

Table 5.1: Simulated Tax Revenue.

Income Tax	**Total Simulated Tax Revenue from 1970 to 2013 (in millions)**										
	25%	**24%**	**23%**	**22%**	**21%**	**20%**	**19%**	**18%**	**17%**	**16%**	**15%**
Wealth Tax											
2.5%											
3%											
3.5%						Total simulated taxes are below the actual total taxes					
4%											
4.5%	1,996,766	1,955,864	1,914,963								
5%	2,105,013	2,064,112	2,023,210	1,982,308							
5.5%	2,213,260	2,172,359	2,131,457	2,090,555	2,049,654	2,008,752	1,967,850	1,926,949			
6%	2,321,507	2,280,606	2,239,704	2,198,802	2,157,901	2,116,999	2,076,097	2,035,196	1,994,294	1,953,392	
6.5%	2,429,755	2,388,853	2,347,951	2,307,049	2,266,148	2,225,246	2,184,344	2,143,443	2,102,541	2,061,639	2,020,738
7%	2,538,002	2,497,100	2,456,198	2,415,297	2,374,395	2,333,493	2,292,592	2,251,690	2,319,035	2,169,886	2,128,985
7.5%	2,646,249	2,605,347	2,564,445	2,523,544	2,482,642	2,441,740	2,400,839	2,359,937	2,427,282	2,278,134	2,237,232
8%	2,754,496	2,713,594	2,672,692	2,631,791	2,590,889	2,549,987	2,509,086	2,468,184	2,535,529	2,386,381	2,345,479
8.5%	2,862,743	2,821,841	2,780,940	2,740,038	2,699,136	2,658,234	2,617,333	2,576,431	2,643,777	2,494,628	2,453,726
9%	2,970,990	2,930,088	2,889,187	2,848,285	2,807,383	2,766,482	2,725,580	2,684,678	2,752,024	2,602,875	2,561,973
9.5%	3,079,237	3,038,335	2,997,434	2,956,532	2,915,630	2,874,729	2,833,827	2,792,925	2,948,278	2,711,122	2,670,220
10%	3,187,484	3,146,583	3,105,681	3,064,779	3,023,877	2,982,976	2,942,074	2,901,172	2,860,271	2,819,369	2,778,467
Viable tax rate combination	25% &4.5%	24% &4.5%	23% &4.5%	22%&5%	21% &5.5%	20% &5.5%	19% &5.5%	18% &5.5%	17%&6%	16%&6%	15% &6.5%

Note: The highlighted figures indicate the total simulated tax revenue that is higher than the total actual tax revenue for the periods 1970 to 2013 using the minimum combination of tax rate. Any of these combinations of income and wealth tax rates can be considered as the viable tax rates. The final tax rate combination selected is based on the combination of tax rates that give the most total tax revenue among the viable combination.

5.2.2 New Government Expenditure

The simulated government expenditure is a simple accounting procedure undertaken on the actual government expenditure, government debt and interest payment for the period from 1970 to 2013. The proposed fiscal structure finances government development expenditure, and any deficit during the year via issuance of Equity Participation Shares (EPS) that are issued in low denominations to the general public. The EPS is a risk sharing instrument whereby the general public participates in a portfolio of development projects undertaken by the government. Instead of financing these projects through interest-bearing borrowings, the government utilizes the idle funds available in the public sector or funds being deposited in low-return savings accounts through the issuance of EPS to finance the development projects. The main attractive feature of the EPS is that the return on the EPS is benchmarked against the real rate of return of the projects. If the rate of return on the economy of approximately 5% is taken as an example of the return to the investors of the EPS, the return received by them is definitely higher than the return on the money deposited in the savings account by 2%–3%. By issuing EPS, the government borrowing will be reduced over the years as the existing debts retire. The expenditure on interest rate will also be correspondingly reduced hence improving the government budgetary position. The cost of interest payment released from the reduction in borrowing can be used to finance any shortfall in subsequent years' government budget. That means the new government expenditure comprises of the operating expenditure of the government and the revised debt service payments. The result of the new government expenditure (*NGG*) is shown in the plot of a graph against the existing government expenditure (*GG*) in Figure 5.2.

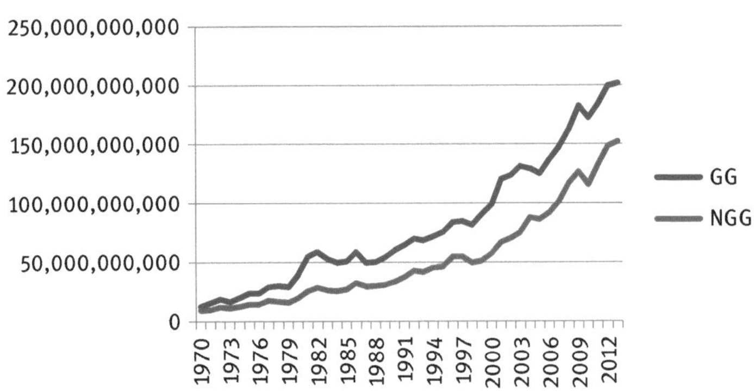

Figure 5.2: Actual and New Government Expenditure.

Similar to government revenue, the trend of government expenditure under the existing and proposed fiscal framework is approximately the same upward trend, except that *GG* is rising at a faster rate than *NGG*. The graph above shows that *NGG* is consistently lower as compared to *G*. Under the existing fiscal condition, government debt has been on the rise due to the financing of persistent budget deficits. As the financing is interest rate-based, the debt service is a burden to the government's now rising operating expenditure. Conversely, the new fiscal structure progressively reduces the debt burden by financing government expenditure through participation from the public and private sector – hence the lower *NGG*. The time series of government expenditure obtained using the accounting adjustment of the government finances as explained above is used in the econometric tests as new government expenditure (*NGG*).

5.3 Index of Fiscal Sustainability

Many studies done on fiscal sustainability has chosen one of two methods of fiscal assessment, i.e. the fiscal indicator or fiscal sustainability test. This study has adopted both methodologies in order to assess the fiscal sustainability of Malaysia.

Equation (8b) of section 4.3.1 of the previous chapter explained the derivation of the fiscal sustainability indicator (FSI), which is replicated below:

$$FSI_t = (\beta_t - \lambda_t) = \left(\frac{1+r_t}{1+g_t} - \frac{ps_t - ps^*}{d_{t-1} - d^*}\right)$$

The value of FSI_t below 1, that is $| \beta_t - \lambda_t | < 1$, indicates a sustainable fiscal position while values consistently above or equal to 1 indicate unsustainability. The FSI is calculated recursively from the year 1980 to 2013 using the actual data and the simulated data, and a summary of the results are presented in Table 5.2.

Table 5.2: Summary of FSI Result and Its Components.

	Existing Fiscal Policy	Proposed Fiscal Policy
	Frequency	
$\beta > \lambda$	41.2%	14.7%
$\beta > \beta^*$	32.4%	35.2%
$\lambda < 0$	55.9%	0.09%

Table 5.2 reveals that the frequency of FSI being more than 1 is higher under the existing fiscal framework. The same can be said about the frequency of λ assuming a negative value. The frequency of high values of β under both fiscal frameworks are almost the same. However, the frequency of negative values of λ is higher than the frequency of high values of $\beta > \beta^*$ under the existing fiscal framework. This indicates that improving the fiscal stance as measured by λ matters as compared to the effect of interest rate in β. More often than not, the high interest rate might not affect

the stock of debt immediately, and improvements in the fiscal stance might lead to future improvements in the interest rate and growth gap (Croce & Juan-Ramón, 2003). Figure 5.3 is the plot of the FSI under existing fiscal framework.

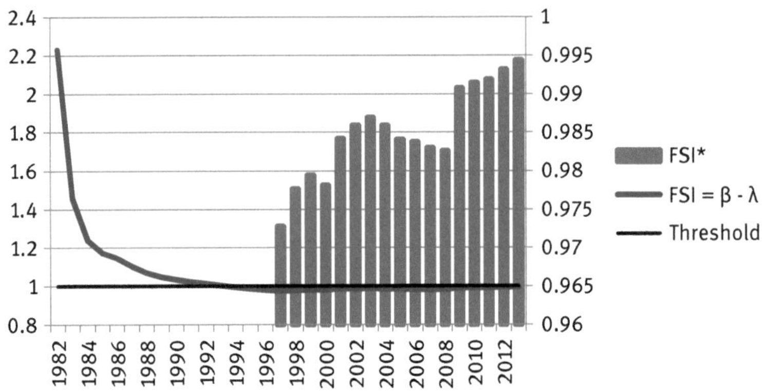

Figure 5.3: Fiscal Sustainability Index Under the Existing Fiscal Policy.

The above figure shows that fiscal policy has been sustainable where the FSI moved below unity in 1995 and remained so until the present. The bar chart of FSI* magnifies the trend of FSI from the year 1997 onwards to show its robustness and sustainability. As shown by FSI*, the fiscal sustainability of Malaysia has deteriorated in recent years as it moves towards unity. Mapping the FSI against the fiscal deficit situation of Malaysia, the sustainability indicator seems to be consistent with Malaysia's budget surplus position between the years 1993 to 1997. It is interesting to note that during the Asian financial crisis of 1997/1998, the FSI continues to indicate a sustainable fiscal position for Malaysia. The Malaysian economy seemed to be able to sustain through the Asian financial crisis due to the strong budget position in the years preceding the crisis. Even though FSI continues to indicate positive fiscal sustainability throughout the subsequent financial crisis in 2007/2008, the fiscal stance was not strong enough to maintain a strong sustainability position. As can be seen in the FSI* bar chart, the index started to move upwards towards unity, indicating a deteriorating sustainability position from 2008 onwards.

Let's now compare Figure 5.3 to the FSI' under the proposed fiscal framework as shown in the Figure 5.4.

The sustainability position continues to improve starting from 1985, as shown by the downward trend in the FSI'. This is due to improving fiscal stance over the years arising from the increased government revenue and at the same time decreasing government expenditure under the proposed fiscal structure. As the primary surplus figure improves, the value of λ will improve in tandem thereby reducing the value of FSI' further below unity, indicating an improving fiscal sustainability position.

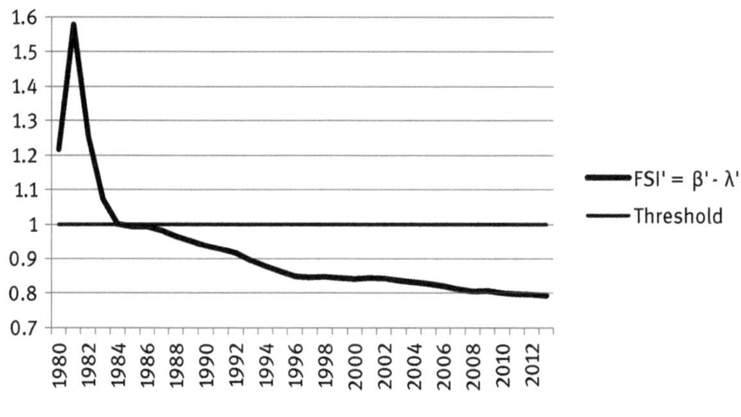

Figure 5.4: Fiscal Sustainability Index Under Proposed Fiscal Policy.

5.4 Sustainability Test

A sustainability test that analyses the relationship between government revenue and government expenditure is carried out not only to corroborate or otherwise, the results of the fiscal sustainability index but further tests using Dynamic OLS will also determine the merit of one fiscal framework from another. The sustainability test involves determining the unit root of government revenue (*R*) and government expenditure (*GG*) and subsequently testing the existence of a long run relationship between *R* and *GG*. Following Martin, (2000), the deficit situation is "strongly" sustainable if the I(1) process of *R* and *GG* are cointegrated with a coefficient, $\beta = 1$. If *R* and *GG* are cointegrated and $0 < \beta < 1$, the fiscal position is "weakly" sustainable. In carrying out the tests, it is assumed that the real interest rate is stationary around its mean. The same tests are replicated on *GG* and *NR*, *R* and *NGG* and *NR* and *NGG* to check for sustainability under the proposed fiscal framework.

5.4.1 Univariate Unit Root Tests

A variable is stationary when its mean, variance and covariance are constant over time. To check for stationarity, the Augmented Dickey-Fuller (ADF) test, GLS-based Dickey-Fuller (DF-GLS) and Phillips-Perron (PP) tests are used. In addition, the Zivot-Andrews (Z-A) test is used to detect a unit root in a time series with unknown structural break. Table 5.3 displays the empirical results of the unit root tests performed on *GG*,[49] *R*, *NR* and *NGG*.

The null hypothesis, H_0 is that the variable has a unit root. All the testing procedures suggest the existence of unit root in level or I(0) series of *R*, *GG*, *NR* and *NGG*.

49 Note: $GG_t = G_t + i_t D_{t-1}$ and $NGG_t = NG_t + i_t D_{t-1}$

Table 5.3: Results of Unit Root and Stationarity Test.

	LEVEL			Z-A	FIRST DIFFERENCES			Z-A
	ADF	ADF-GLS	PP		ADF	ADF-GLS	PP	
GG	−0.812(0)	−0.936(0)	−0.426(6)	−2.538(0) [2006]	−4.755***(3)	−6.318***(0)	−6.829***(12)	−6.155***(3) [1987]
R	−1.399(0)	−1.457(0)	−1.045(7)	−2.939(0) [2006]	−4.944***(3)	−5.094***(3)	−10.344***(18)	−5.917***(3) [1998]
NGG	2.332(9)	−1.218(9)	3.393(42)	−0.147(2) [2006]	−7.413***(1)	−7.435***(1)	−9.518***(33)	−8.809***(1) [2001]
NR	−0.848(3)	−1.237(3)	−1.059(4)	−2.293(3) [2006]	−3.609**(5)	−3.099*(2)	−8.562***(3)	−4.921*(5) [1997]

Note: All tests include intercept and linear trend (except Z-A test with only intercept). Asterisks *,**,*** denote level of significance at 10%, 5% and 1% respectively. Figures in ( ) are the lag length and the figures in [] are the break point for Z-A test. Except for *NGG*, which uses the Schwarz Information Criterion (SIC), the lag length is chosen using Akaike Information Criterion (AIC) for the ADF and ADF-GLS tests by setting the maximum lag length as nine, and the Newey-West Bandwidth using Bartlett Kernel for the PP test. The maximum lag length for all variables set for the Z-A test is eight with the exception of maximum lag length of two for *NG*. The asymptotic and finite sample critical values for ADF and PP tests is obtained from Mackinnon, (1996) and from Elliot, Rothenberg, & Stock, (1996) for ADF-GLS test.

By first-differencing the series, the non-stationary component is removed. After performing this procedure on the series under consideration, the test report in the table suggests that the null hypothesis of non-stationarity is clearly rejected at the 1% significance level for all variables except for *NR* whose significance level varies according to the different tests. Therefore, it can be concluded that all variables *R*, *GG*, *NR* and *NGG* are integrated of order 1 or I(1) series.

5.4.2 Cointegration Relationship

According to Hakkio & Rush (1991), if government expenditure and revenue series contain a unit root (i.e. integrated of order 1) then the long-run relationship between them can be determined. If such relationship does not exist, then debt would be unsustainable. The finding that all the variables of interest above have the same order of integration allows the study to proceed with the Johansen multivariate cointegration analysis. Cointegrating relationship is the convergence of two or more non-stationary time series in the long run. The cointegration test used is based on the maximum likelihood estimation that proposes two distinct tests for determining likelihood ratios, which are trace and maximum eigenvalue statistics. The null hypothesis is that there is no cointegrating vector, r, i.e. the value of r is 0.

Unit root tests for actual government revenue and expenditure and the simulated government revenue and expenditure. Sample period is from 1970 to 2013.

This study performed a two-step test to determine the existence of cointegration relationship. Firstly, the Johansen cointegration test is performed on the variables *GG* and *R*, *GG* and *NR*, *R* and *NGG*, *NGG* and *NR* by employing the specification that there are no linear time trends on the levels of data. The results in Table 5.4 show that the null hypothesis of no cointegration vector is rejected in favour of at least one cointegration vector at the 5% level of significance. Secondly, the study employs the unit root test for the budget deficit *BD (GG – R)*. According to Trehan & Walsh (1991), the unit root test for *BD* is comparable to the test of the cointegrating relationship between *GG* and *R* (Miyazaki, 2014; Neaime, 2015). The same test is also applied to *NBD*. The results are reported in Table 5.5. The test results show that the stationarity of budget balance, *BD* and *NBD* are confirmed.

Table 5.4 shows a cointegrating relationship or a long-run time trending pattern between government expenditure and government revenue in both the actual and simulated data. Therefore, it can be concluded that under all the following scenarios, the fiscal stance is sustainable:

1. The existing fiscal condition in Malaysia.
2. Fiscal policy under the proposed flat tax system.
3. Fiscal policy based on interest-free government financing.
4. A proposed fiscal framework comprising a flat tax system and interest-free government financing.

Cointegration tests for actual government revenue and expenditure and the simulated government revenue and expenditure. Sample period is from 1970 to 2013.

Table 5.4: Results of Johansen Cointegration Test.

NULL	ALTERNATIVE		TEST STATISTICS		
Hypothesis (GG and R)			**Critical Value**		**Critical Value**
H_0	H_1	**Trace**	**5%**	**Max-Eigen**	**5%**
$r = 0 r \leq 1$	$r \geq 1 r = 2$	23.1108** 6.6055	20.2618 9.1645	16.5054** 6.6055	15.8921 9.1645
Hypothesis (*GG* and *NR*)		**Critical Value**		**Critical Value**	
H_0	H_1	**Trace**	**5%**	**Max-Eigen**	**5%**
$r = 0 r \leq 1$	$r \geq 1 r = 2$	30.2838** 7.7566	20.26184 9.16455	22.5271** 7.7566	15.8921 9.16455
Hypothesis (*R* and *NGG*)		**Critical Value**		**Critical Value**	
H_0	H_1	**Trace**	**5%**	**Max-Eigen**	**5%**
$r = 0 r \leq 1$	$r \geq 1 r = 2$	34.4363** 5.5639	20.2618 9.1645	28.8725** 5.5639	15.8921 9.14555
Hypothesis (*NGG* and *NR*)			**Critical Value**		**Critical Value**
H_0	H_1	**Trace**	**5%**	**Max-Eigen**	**5%**
$r = 0 r \leq 1$	$r \geq 1 r = 2$	32.5759** 6.9324	20.2618 9.16455	25.6436** 6.9324	15.8921 9.16455

Note: The test assumes no deterministic trend in the data but include an intercept. Asterisks ** indicates rejection of the hypothesis at the 5% significance level. The lag length is one for *GG* and *R*, three for *NGG* and *R* and *NGG* and *NR* based on sequential modified LR test statistics for all cases, and four for *GG* and *NR* based on AIC.

Unit root tests for the actual and simulated budget balances. Sample period is from 1970 to 2013.

In addition, Table 5.5 shows that the existing budget balance (*BD*= *R* – *GG*) under scenario 1 above has unit root when tested under ADF, ADF-GLS and PP but is stationary in first difference, that is integrated of order one, I(1). However, it is integrated of order zero, I(0) according to the Z-A test. With the presence of a structural break, it can be shown that the null hypothesis of unit root for *BD* can be rejected. According to Trehan & Walsh (1991), this constitutes a sufficient condition to conclude that a fiscal policy is sustainable. This means that the government deficit will not grow without bounds and the actual deficit will asymptotically converge to zero over time. The budget balance for the simulated data (*NBD*= *NR* – *NGG*) on the other hand is integrated of order 1, I(1) for all unit root tests. Hence, following Hakkio & Rush (1991), in cases when the two

Table 5.5: Results of Unit Root Test for Budget Balance.

	LEVEL				FIRST DIFFERENCE			
	ADF	ADF-GLS	PP	Z-A	ADF	ADF-GLS	PP	Z-A
BD	−1.574(1)	−1.4115(1)	−1.574(1)	−3.772***(1) [1987]	−5.353***(0)	−5.366***(0)	−5.353***(0)	
NBD	−0.0724(2)	−0.3743(3)	−1.149(4)	−3.461(3) [1993]	−8.8174***(1)	−8.920***(1)	−9.372***(2)	−10.583***(1) [1997]

Note: All tests include intercept. Asterisks *,**,*** denote level of significance at 10%, 5% and 1% respectively. Figures in ( ) are the lag length and the figures in [] are the break point for Z-A test. The lag length is set at the maximum lag length of eight.

series (in this case *NR* and *NGG* that makes up *NBD*) contain unit root (i.e. integrated of order 1) then the next step is to search for a long-run equilibrium relationship between the series. If such a relationship exists, then the budget deficit is sustainable. The results of the cointegration test on *NR* and *NGG* in Table 5.4 shows that such long-run equilibrium relationship exists. As such, it can be concluded that the fiscal stance under the proposed fiscal regime (scenario 4 above) is also sustainable.

The break points given by the Z-A test in Table 5.5 suggests that there is a structural break in the time series. The break point of 1987 indicated for *BD* is consistent with the widespread stock market crash ("Black Monday") in October 1987. It can also be noted that the break point given for *NBD* coincides with the Asian financial crisis in the late 1990s. In estimating the cointegration vector, it is therefore legitimate to include a structural break.

5.5 Estimation of Long-Run Equilibria

So far, the empirical results have shown that fiscal policy under all the four scenarios stated in Section 4.2 above is sustainable. Given that government expenditure and revenue are cointegrated, the study then estimates the model for the sample period under all the four scenarios using DOLS. The DOLS is used to test whether the cointegration coefficient of equation (20), $\beta_1 = 1$ (strong form of sustainability condition) or is no significant difference from 1. The Wald test is used to determine whether the null hypotheses that $\beta_1 = \beta_2 = D_f = 0$ is rejected (β_1, β_2, D_f in equation 20). The DOLS is estimated using lead and lag 1. To check the robustness of the DOLS estimates, the model is re-estimated by increasing the lead and lag.

5.5.1 DOLS without Structural Break

The study will firstly estimate the parameters without considering structural break. The DOLS equations are as follows:

$$R_t = \alpha + \beta GG_t + \sum_{j=-p}^{p} \gamma_j GG_{t-j} + \mu_t \qquad \text{Scenario1}$$

$$NR_t = \alpha + \hat{\beta} GG_t + \sum_{j=-p}^{p} \hat{\gamma}_j GG_{t-j} + \hat{\mu}_t \qquad \text{Scenario2}$$

$$R_t = \alpha + \tilde{\beta} NGG_t + \sum_{j=-p}^{p} \tilde{\gamma}_j NGG_{t-j} + \tilde{\mu}_t \qquad \text{Scenario3}$$

$$NR_t = \alpha + \bar{\beta} NGG_t + \sum_{j=-p}^{p} \bar{\gamma}_j NGG_{t-j} + \bar{\mu}_t \qquad \text{Scenario4}$$

The results of the DOLS estimate without a structural break for *NR* and *GG* (scenario 2) and *R* and *NGG* (scenario 3) are presented in Table 5.6, and for *R* and *GG* (scenario 1) and *NR* and *NGG* (scenario 4) are presented in Table 5.7.

Table 5.6: Results of Dynamic OLS Estimation Without Structural Break for NR-GG and R-NGG.

	Dependent Variable	**NR**			**R**		
Lags & Leads	**Independent Variable**	$\widehat{\beta}$	**Wald Statistics**	$\overline{R}^2$	$\widetilde{\beta}$	**Wald Statistics**	$\overline{R}^2$
1	***GG***	1.0969***	12.6362***	0.9245			
		(0.0868)					
2	***GG***	1.1156***	11.4740***	0.9201			
		(0.1222)					
3	***GG***	1.1657***	7.4036***	0.9047			
		(0.1575)					
1	***NGG***				1.1448***	9.0309***	0.9499
					(0.1268)		
2	***NGG***				1.1977***	5.5168***	0.9410
					(0.2171)		
3	***NGG***				1.3719***	4.8590***	0.9370
					(0.2823)		

Note: Figures in () are the standard errors. Asterisks *** indicates significance at 1%. The above shows the results for scenarios 2 (NR-GG) and 3 (R-NGG).

Table 5.7: Results of Dynamic OLS Estimation Without Structural Break for R-GG and NR-NGG.

	Dependent Variable	**R**			**NR**		
Lags & Leads	**Independent Variable**	β	**Wald Statistics**	$\overline{R}^2$	$\overline{\beta}$	**Wald Statistics**	$\overline{R}^2$
1	***GG***	0.8452***	16.2616***	0.9651			
		(0.0520)					
2	***GG***	0.8650***	11.4740***	0.9579			
		(0.0754)					
3	***GG***	0.8945***	9.2334***	0.9484			
		(0.0969)					
1	***NGG***				1.5023***	10.3801***	0.9429
					(0.1447)		
2	***NGG***				1.4465***	5.2778***	0.9275
					(0.2740)		
3	***NGG***				1.7217***	5.0581***	0.9387
					(0.3404)		

Note: Figures in () are the standard errors. Asterisks *** indicates significance at 1%. The above shows the results for scenarios 1 (R-GG) and 4 (NR-NGG).

The results show that the coefficients estimated are statistically significant at a 1% confidence interval. It can be seen that the values of $\hat{\beta}$, $\tilde{\beta}$ and $\bar{\beta}$ are well above 1 as compared to the value of β, indicating stronger form fiscal sustainability under the scenarios where fiscal reform is introduced. The value of the coefficient is highest (ie $\bar{\beta}$) when a comprehensive fiscal reform is introduced as in scenario 4 (that incorporates fiscal reforms in scenarios 2 and 3). Therefore, from here onwards, the study will focus on comparing the existing fiscal framework (scenario 1) and the proposed fiscal framework under scenario 4.

5.5.2 DOLS with Structural Break

Based on the tests that include a break done on *BD* and *NBD* earlier, there may be a structural change in the relationship between *GG* and *R* in 1987 and between *NGG* and *NR* in 1997. To confirm the structural break, Figure 5.5 shows the plot of budget deficit to GDP ratio for both the actual and simulated data, represented by *bd* and *nbd* respectively.

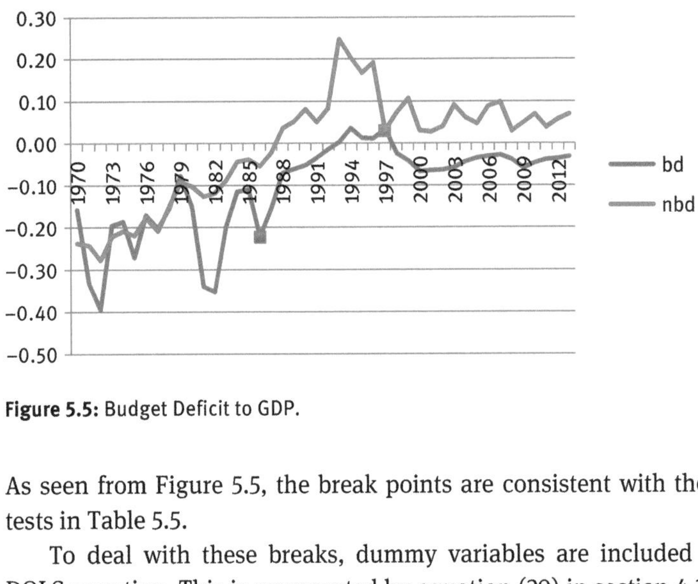

Figure 5.5: Budget Deficit to GDP.

As seen from Figure 5.5, the break points are consistent with the result of the Z-A tests in Table 5.5.

To deal with these breaks, dummy variables are included in estimating the DOLS equation. This is represented by equation (20) in section 4.3.4 in the previous chapter and the equation is reproduced below for *R* and *GG* (scenario 1):

$$R_t = \alpha + D_{f1} + \beta_1 GG_t + \beta_2 (D_{f1}{}^* \, GG_t) + \sum_{j=-p}^{p} \gamma_j GG_{t-j} + \sum_{j=-p}^{p} \delta_j \, (D_{f1}{}^* \, GG_{t-j}) + \mu_t$$

Similarly, the equation for *NR* and *NGG* (scenario 4) is as follows:

$$NR_t = \alpha + D_{f2} + \beta_3 NGG_t + \beta_4 (D_{f2}{}^* NGG_t) + \sum_{j=-p}^{p} \gamma_j NGG_{t-j} + \sum_{j=-p}^{p} \delta_j (D_{f2}{}^* NGG_{t-j}) + \mu_t$$

The Wald test is used to determine whether the null hypotheses that $D_{f1} = \beta_1 = \beta_2 = 0$ and $D_{f2} = \beta_3 = \beta_4 = 0$ are rejected. Similar to the above, to check the robustness of the DOLS estimates, the model is re-estimated by increasing the lead and lag to 2 and 3. The results of DOLS with structural break are presented in Table 5.8.

Based on the DOLS estimation, the coefficients of the independent variables *GG* and *NGG* are statistically significant at the 1% confidence interval for all lead and lag order except *NGG* at lead and lag 3. The coefficients of the interaction term however are not significant under both fiscal frameworks. The value of coefficients β_1 (with inclusion of structural break) and β (without structural break) are below 1 with $\beta_1 < \beta$. These results are consistent in concluding the existence of a weak form of sustainability under the current fiscal framework. On the other hand, the value of coefficients under the proposed fiscal framework is above 1 (except for β_3 in the case of lead and lag 3 under the structural break condition) with $\beta_3 < \bar{\beta}$ suggesting a strong form of fiscal sustainability.

In addition, it is also shown that the coefficients β_2 and β_4 for the interaction terms between the dummies and *GG* and *NGG*, are not statistically significant and negative for β_2. This means the presence of the interaction terms as regressors has little bearing to the model. However, the Wald test results reject the null of $D_{f1} = \beta_1 = \beta_2 = 0$ and $D_{f2} = \beta_3 = \beta_4 = 0$, which confirms that structural changes took place, both in the intercept and slope parameters. The empirical evidence supports the conclusion that fiscal stance is more sustainable under the proposed fiscal framework where the value of $\bar{\beta}$, β_3 (for lead and lag 1 and 2) > 1 compared to the existing fiscal situation. Even though the results of the fiscal sustainability test in Section 5.4 corroborates the sustainability conclusion given by the FSI in Section 5.3, this section shows that the sustainability condition is only "weakly" sustainable. Again, this weak form of sustainability is consistent with the conclusion obtained from the FSI as shown in Figure 5.3.

The results for the proposed fiscal policy reveal that government revenue is growing at a faster rate than government expenditure. For example, for every Ringgit spent on expenditure, government revenue can increase up to RM1.72. This suggests that the revenue generated from efficient tax collection are more than able to cover the expenditures incurred by the government, which can in turn contribute to a strong performance of the government's financial accounts. The interaction between government revenue and expenditure can be examined further using causality analysis.

Based on the results above, there is a bi-directional long run causation or relationship between *GG* and *R*, and *NGG* and *NR*. However, in the short run, there is no causality between *R* and *GG*, which means the authorities can set the level of expenditure and revenue by rule of thumb. In the short run, there is a one-way causation from *NR* to *NGG*, which means the authorities adjust their expenditure according to the level of revenue. The long-run causality results seem to suggest that the authorities make simultaneous decisions on expenditure and revenues or fiscal synchronization and the two variables mutually support each other. This hypothesis is based on the equivalence of marginal cost and marginal revenue that the utility-maximising suppliers and demanders of the public services make (Baharumshah & Lau, 2007). This is true, as every year the government presents the Budget for the next year by tabling the planned expenditure together with changes in taxes or tax rates. Based on the equations above, government expenditure has a higher effect for every change in government revenue, as opposed to the effect government revenue has for every change in government expenditure. This is true under both the existing and proposed fiscal frameworks. However, the magnitude of the effect of revenue on expenditure of 2.6627 is higher under the proposed fiscal framework compared to 1.2477 under the existing fiscal framework. This implies that the change in government expenditure under the proposed fiscal framework generates a higher amount of revenue to the government compared to the existing fiscal framework.

5.7 Analysis of Results

The first question on the sustainability of Malaysia's existing fiscal policy is addressed by the results in Sections 5.3 and 5.4. The results of the FSI are corroborated by the results of the fiscal sustainability tests in Sections 5.4.1 and 5.4.2, which shows that the current fiscal position of Malaysia is sustainable. The effect of the introduction of a proposed reform in the tax structure and the way government finances its expenditure on fiscal sustainability are addressed in the same sections. Additionally, Sections 5.5.1 and 5.5.2 show that the impact on sustainability is better compared to the existing fiscal situation.

Further tests by DOLS show that this sustainability condition is a weak form of sustainability under the existing fiscal framework as compared to the strong sustainability given by the value of parameter of the equation that is above unity under the proposed fiscal framework. In addition, the causality analysis confirms that the proposed fiscal framework is better in terms of generating revenue for the government.

The results of this study presented above are consistent with previous studies done by Baharumshah & Lau (2007) and Abdullah, et. al. (2012). The result of the sustainability index shows that the fiscal sustainability of Malaysia under the current situation is sustainable even though the sustainability is weakening. Malaysia has had strong economic growth over the years, except in the year following the

Asian financial and sub-prime crises. The GDP growth of Malaysia has been at a steady rate of 5% to 10%. Malaysia emerged from both the financial crises with a better growth rate – averaging at 5%, compared to its neighbouring countries. Malaysia was able to ride through the Asian financial crisis, as its external borrowing then comprised a smaller portion of its total borrowing; coupled with strong economic fundamentals and healthy investment activities. These fundamentals have enabled Malaysia to withstand the accretion of its debt over the years.

However, this position of high debt and persistent deficits cannot be sustainable in the long run, as illustrated by the FSI in the last 10 years. There have been many articles written and studies carried out on the effect of debt on the economy (Arcand, et al., 2012; Baum, et.al., 2013; Lima, et al., 2008; Reinhart & Rogoff, 2009) that lends support to the justification that the increasing debt in Malaysia – which affects the primary surplus and debt ratio in the FSI – is one of the contributing factors to the deteriorating fiscal sustainability condition in Malaysia. A study by Baum et al., (2013) suggests that there is a positive short-run impact of debt on GDP growth. This positive impact decreases as the debt to GDP ratio increases to around 67%. For debt to GDP ratio that exceeds 95%, additional debt has a negative impact on economic activity as the long-term interest rate is subject to increased pressure. Reinhart & Rogoff (2009, 2010) found that when debt rose above 90% of GDP, some sort of 'tipping point' was reached whereby country growth slowed down after the 90% line was crossed. Therefore, the effect of rising debts cannot be disregarded if the fiscal sustainability needs to be kept in check.

It should also be noted that the debt figures that have been used in this study are the government debt figures in terms of its own borrowing. Any contingent liabilities, such as guarantees given by the government on debts taken by other government-related entities have not been taken into account. This contingent liability, if materializes, will affect the debt to GDP ratio of the country unfavourably. Negative market sentiments have already impacted foreign investment interests, the value of Malaysian currency, as well as the stock market.

Both the DOLS and ECM results above are consistent in suggesting that the proposed fiscal framework is better in ensuring fiscal sustainability. The value of the coefficients of the independent variables is higher under the proposed framework than the existing framework in both tests. These results empirically confirm the positive effect of improved government revenue and reduced expenditure under the proposed fiscal framework as depicted in Figures 5.1 and 5.2. Additionally, the much reduced budget deficit as shown in Figure 5.5 also confirms the expectation of an improved fiscal sustainability. Therefore, economic intuition suggests that the authorities should look into reforming the tools of fiscal policy either through the tax structure or government financing policy, as shown in the results in Section 5.5 or both.

5.8 Conclusion

This chapter provides an empirical analysis of the fiscal sustainability of Malaysia under different scenarios, while at the same time assessing the viability of a proposed fiscal framework. The core findings of this chapter point towards a robust argument in favour of a new holistic approach in improving the fiscal sustainability of Malaysia. Even though the empirical results show that the current fiscal position is sustainable, its sustainability may be threatened in the near future – especially under lackluster economic conditions. The study proposes a new tax structure based on a flat rate tax system that is easier to administer and an interest-free government financing that eases the government's burden on borrowing. This proposal addresses the low tax revenue collection and the rising debt ratio of the country. At the same time, the proposed policy looks at the best interest of the public and enhancing cooperation between the public and the government.

6 Policy Recommendation

6.1 Introduction

This study is probably the first empirical work that looks at an alternative way of improving the fiscal stance in Malaysia. This study began with the assessment of fiscal sustainability for Malaysia under the existing fiscal framework whereby the tax system is based on multiple types of taxes and progressive income tax, and the public sector financing is based on interest rate debt instruments. Utilizing two types of fiscal sustainability assessments, the fiscal position of Malaysia was empirically shown to be sustainable. However, the fiscal sustainability indicator showed that the sustainability of the Malaysian fiscal framework has weakened in recent years. Similar fiscal assessments were applied to the time series of simulated data on tax revenue and government expenditure, which is based on a proposed fiscal framework comprising a flat rate tax system on income and wealth only, and a public sector financing policy that utilizes equity participation shares issued to the general public. It was empirically shown that under the proposed fiscal framework, the fiscal sustainability is stronger. This was indicated by the results of the fiscal sustainability indicator that gradually moves further below unity over time. The fiscal sustainability test corroborated the above findings. The coefficients of the DOLS equation of more than 1 under the proposed fiscal framework showed that the fiscal sustainability of the proposed framework is stronger than the existing fiscal framework which shows a positive coefficient but value of below 1. Therefore, it can be concluded that a case for fiscal reform is justifiable.

Rather than looking at the conventional policy prescriptions in alleviating the budgetary imbalance, such as introducing new or increasing taxes, or introducing expenditure restriction or fiscal stimulus, it is time that policymakers take a holistic approach in reforming the way fiscal policy tools are used in stabilizing the economy. The proposals for reform suggested by this book are based on the objective of improving the current impediments in the fiscal tools. Among the issues raised relating to the long-term sustainability of the Malaysian economy are;

1. Sufficiency of tax revenue to cover government expenditure
2. Perceived injustice brought about by the current tax system
3. Adverse distributional impact as a result of rising government debt

The fiscal framework proposed in this book seeks to bring about three main benefits: firstly, positive distributional impact, secondly, good governance, and thirdly, economic resilience.

https://doi.org/10.1515/9783110591187-006

6.2 Role of the Government and Policy Design

One of the most important roles of the government is the design and implementation of incentive structures that encourage coordination and cooperation in the market to achieve a desired economic goal. These incentive structures are incorporated in government policies that should create a just and equitable outcome for all.

Usually, government objectives for the economy are stability and material growth. In market economies, the government does this by taking actions that affect private sector portfolios – in terms of consumption and investment. In recent years, there has been more emphasis on attaining economic well-being. This means economic growth should not be at the expense of deteriorating quality of life and equity for the players in the economy. In the wake of the recent financial crisis for example, astronomical sums of public tax money have been poured into the affected economies to avert a complete breakdown. Whether or not bailouts are justified, the risk of reckless leveraging for high private profits was shifted ultimately to taxpayers, as they have had to bear the costs. In the process, economic justice has suffered. This is currently being experienced in Malaysia. The implementation of a new consumption tax, GST, in 2015 was seen by many as a consequence of mismanagement in spending by the government and bail out of ailing government-linked companies.

A policy design that favors a rich minority over an increasingly impoverished majority is not a credible economic policy for social equality. If the social aspects of economic growth are a matter of central concern, then the adequacy and appropriateness of the policies currently being implemented to regulate the economy need to be reviewed. The weaknesses in the current system can be pinned down to policies and practices that encourage excessive creation of debt and pay little attention to the social and ethical aspects of market practices (Othman & Mirakhor, 2013). Therefore, the author is of the opinion that an ideal fiscal policy would be one that embraces the following attributes:

- Social justice and equity with more equitable distribution of income
- Trust and transparency
- Cooperation and coordination through sharing of risks
- Finance grounded in the real economy

The current fiscal situation in Malaysia where high levels of debt and persistent deficits constraint the government's ability to effectively respond to future shocks is the impetus for reform. Any additional borrowings will not only burden the present but also future generations. This is due to the fact that the middle- and lower-income classes carry the burden of the taxes that are needed to service government debt, held by either the higher income groups or foreign creditors. One of the thrusts of the 10MP and the Shared Prosperity Vision is the reduction of disparity between the poorest and the wealthiest. The mean monthly gross household income has increased from RM6,958 in 2016 to RM7,901 in 2019.[50] There has also emerged a fairly strong middle class. However, incomes are still distributed unevenly. For instance, the top 20% earners among Malaysians earn approximately 47% more monthly income than the rest of the population. The Top 20% (T20) of the population enjoy a better growth in income where the median and mean grew by 4.5% and 4.7% respectively as compared to the growth of the Bottom 40% (B40) which only grew by 1.8% and 3.4% respectively. The median income ratio of the T20 and B40 has also increased by 4.38 times in 2016 to 4.84% in 2019 while mean income increased by 5.65 times in 2016 to 5.87 times in 2019. Under the current tax system that favours the rich, new taxes and/or reduction in subsidies worsen the income inequality.

6.3 Leveraging on The Strength of Islamic Finance Principles

Social justice and equity, trust and transparency, risk sharing and finance grounded in the real economy are all foundations of Islamic finance (a brief write-up on Islamic worldview of the economy is provided in Appendix D). Malaysia has had considerable success in Islamic finance and now recognized as the international center for Islamic finance not only in this region, but globally. For the last 35 years, Malaysia has developed an impressive Islamic financial system that operates alongside the conventional system. A comprehensive Islamic framework and legislation as well as firm regulatory and government support have reinforced both the growth of Islamic banking and the capital market. With the success of Islamic finance in the banking and capital market sector, it is high time that Islamic finance is also embraced in the macroeconomic management of the country.

Risk sharing is the essence of Islamic finance. Lessons from the debt crisis and interest rate-based system force a fundamental reassessment of the way fiscal policy is conducted. Current policies based on the risk transfer system have adverse implications to the economy. Tax policies that consistently burden the poor and middle-class societies (such as GST) will exacerbate the current income and wealth disparity. An alternative approach to reduce the emerging imbalances and the divergence between the financial and real economy is needed. This is where the risk sharing feature of Islamic finance can help bridge the gap.

The Malaysian society is pluralistic – if not in terms of race, language, or ethnicity, then in terms of worldviews, and understanding of values and norms. There must be a spirit of "we are all in it together" in order to maintain a coalition for action. The main success factor is a rule-compliant society. The benefits of emulating Islamic finance principles in macroeconomic policies must be carefully framed and

50 Department of Statistics Household Income and Basic Amenities Survey Report 2019.

economy; ownership of wealth is a significant source of income; the wealthy have more security and access to credit to generate more income and wealth due to their ability to post collateral; wealth owners have more political and economic power that would undermine the basic mechanism of democracy; and where race is intricately tied up with social, political and economic processes such as in Malaysia, unequal distribution of wealth could create serious tensions that could lead to social and political conflicts (Khalid, 2014). In line with the principle in Islam, wealth needs to be circulated so that the benefit accrues to a higher number of people than just the select few in order to achieve economic development.

Based on the above scenario and the current tax structure, it can be seen that tax generation is dampened if the tax structure only taxes income when most of the wealth of the rich is tax-free. The government's imposition of GST will increase the tax base and revenue but at the expense of both the rich and the poor alike. Additionally, with increased borrowing and debt service, the poor will have to bear the burden of higher taxes to pay for the debt instruments held by the rich and the more financially able. This will further increase the disparity between the rich and the poor.

6.5 Risk Sharing Financing

The disturbing consequences of interest-based instruments as highlighted in earlier chapters warrant a rethinking of the current interest-based financial system. The financial crisis and its aftermath have demonstrated the deficiencies in this interest-based system, and the deep macroeconomic roots of the crisis need to be understood in order to draw lessons for the future. Perhaps C. Reinhart & Rogoff (2009) in the book "This Time is Different" have made the most significant contribution to the understanding of the origins of the crisis. They demonstrated that all financial crises ultimately have their origins rooted in one thing – rapid and unsustainable increases in debt. While the specific financial innovations and failures of regulation that contributed to the credit crunch were new, the underlying macroeconomic warning signs were familiar from many previous crises in the past.

Debt-based instruments carries behavioral dimensions and limitations. Current crises and frequent external contagious shocks are caused by pursuing debt-based element that place economies in danger due to the limitations of regulatory debt limit. Furthermore, interest rate has been the anchor of macroeconomic policies. The perception of debt-based instruments as the panacea to economic illness is no longer tenable. The practice of issuing debt-based instruments to generate growth has its limitations, as trust deficit will creep in amongst the debt investors. There will be a tipping point where the debt investors will demand a higher risk premium. Rating agencies are responsible for issuing negative ratings when ratios of debt over GDP have reached internal consensus ceilings. However, critics of credit rating agencies have cited the issue of objectivity as the issuers are paying the agencies. Lack of objectivity may lead to rating agencies issuing lagging or overly aggressive financial reviews of the debt issuer. This can cause a weakening in investor confidence, who will then raise the cost of borrowing and deem financial rescue packages inevitable. All these hampers the ability of economies around the globe to recover and has caused unwanted social displacement.

This book proposes public financing policies that do away with interest rate-based debt. Similar to raising financing through equity, public financing can be done through issuance of risk-sharing instruments such as EPS. The principle of risk sharing also forms the cornerstone of Islamic finance. Islam, in particular, has provided the ways and means by which uncertainties of life can be mitigated. First, it provides a network of rules of behavior and their commensurate payoffs. Complying with these rules reduces uncertainty. Secondly, Islam has provided ways and means for the less able to navigate the uncertainties of life through sharing the risks they face by engaging in economic activities with fellow human beings through exchange.

The moral dimension to risk sharing is its ability to strengthen social solidarity by enhancing cooperation among all economic agents (Askari et al., 2012). Similarly, according to Kharas & Gill (2007), in order for a middle income country like Malaysia to advance out of the middle income status, the benefits of the growing economy must be widely shared, and social opportunity for the vast majority of its citizens must be improved. This is what EPS as a public financing instrument seeks to achieve.

6.6 EPS

The issuance of EPS allows for broader participation of the public in the development and growth of the economy with a return that is closely tied to the real economy. The EPS has to be issued in low denominations so that the general public is able to access it. Current government instruments are only available to institutional investors. The purpose of making EPS available to the general citizen is to tap on the idle funds of the private sector. It allows the investors, who are the general public, to generate a higher return than the current savings rate. This also "breaks down" the role of intermediaries who in the past used depositors' money to subscribe to high return instruments and rewarded the depositors with minimal return.

EPS brings a fresh dimension that combines accountability and participation to all parties involved. Here, the government is bringing development to society by sharing the upside reward of a developmental project back to where the stakeholders' participation interest lies.

Additionally, EPS can be utilised as an instrument for monetary policy. As the EPS is tradable in the secondary market, the liquidity in the economy can be adjusted through the buying and selling of the EPS. In an exercise to contract the money supply, the EPS would be issued directly to the market to mop up excess liquidity. The effect would be more immediate than through the usual transmission mechanism of conventional monetary policy. Conversely, if the goal is to increase money supply, the monetary authority would buy the EPS from the private sector, thus increasing the amount of money in circulation. As a result, expansion in money supply has a much greater chance of resulting in expansion in real production, and thus in employment and income. This is a feature that makes monetary policy far more potent in an interest-free financial system. The combination of the proposed fiscal framework and the use of EPS as a monetary policy instrument is a subject for further research that can contribute to the discourse on Islamic macroeconomic policy.

6.7 Benefits of Policy Recommendations

This book has shown that fiscal consolidation may need to look beyond the usual fiscal measures of increasing taxes and widening the tax base (regardless of ability to pay) and increasing interest-based borrowing (regardless of the distributional implications). A flat tax structure is meant to improve compliance and tax collection. The imposition of tax on wealth presents additional revenue to the government, and most importantly it is a tax imposed on the more able segment of the population. This shifts the burden of higher tax to those who have a higher ability to pay – as opposed to GST, which hits the rich and poor alike.

A financing policy based on a system of risk sharing cultivates a system that promotes financial inclusion instead of supporting the pursuits of certain groups (financially able debt holders) at the cost of others within the society. The partnership between government and the public in development projects will not only mobilise idle private savings in Malaysia to productive use, but also allows private savings – which are currently generating returns of 2% to 3% return, to potentially earn up to 5% to 7% in returns, based on the return to the real sector of the economy.[53] Alternatively, the rate could be benchmarked against the average rate of return to the stock market, which is generally higher than the interest rate in the economy. The cost to the government of raising financing via risk-sharing instruments would not be much higher than the current rate of return paid on debt instruments; instead it provides a better impetus to the growth of the economy by mobilising idle funds.

53 An ISRA Research Paper has come up with an average rate of up to 8.8% as a simulated Islamic pricing benchmark.

6.7.1 Positive Distributional Impact

The imposition of a flat tax rate is able to address some of the impediments of the progressive tax system, which in some circumstances favour the high-income group in Malaysia. The imposition of wealth tax will further help to redistribute income from the rich to the poor. The burden of tax is now distributed based on ability to pay. Additionally, the burden of debt is no longer imposed on the taxpayers, and future generations are safeguarded from shouldering the debt of the current generation by doing away with interest-based financing instruments in public financing policy.

A more equitable opportunity to access the wealth of the nation will be provided to all, regardless of status from the issuance of EPS to the general public. This in turn will further strengthen social solidarity. The EPS provides the public's support to the government in executing projects that are beneficial to the society at large. The positive distribution of wealth achieved is therefore directed to the participating stakeholder's – an opportunity that is lacking under the existing scenario where debt financing is part of the national agenda. This in turn will reduce the oligopolistic nature of rent seekers, financial intermediaries and opportunistic firms.

6.7.2 Good Governance

The importance of good governance has been highlighted all along in the wake of previous financial crises engulfing the Malaysian economy. Ariff (1998) opined that the crises faced by Malaysia were more of a crisis of confidence rather than an economic or financial crisis. For instance, some well-intentioned austerity measures taken by the government in December 1997 might have inadvertently led to an erosion of confidence, as these were seen as ominous signs that the government was experiencing severe financial difficulties. An announcement by Bank Negara Malaysia in January 1998 for the local financial institutions to come up with merger proposals by 31 March 1998 had also adversely impacted market confidence, whereby many in the marketplace saw this as a government effort to bail out the shareholders of weak financial institutions and interpreted the deadline to mean as though the collapse of some banks was imminent. Hence, Ariff (1998) concluded that the origins of the crises were not entirely external. Domestic policies may have also inadvertently contributed to the economic woes of the country. Even with a solid economic foundation, there was a need to recognize policy failures, identify structural flaws in the system and set the house in order.

Public participation in financing development expenditure along with the government, as proposed in the fiscal reform, can enhance the governance structure of the government, as the government will be more accountable to the general public on their development spending. Under this public-government partnership, it is important for strong parliamentary legislative oversight to be put in place. This is to ensure that the government will not keep building deficits and overspend the public funds. As the pricing of the EPS is left to the prevailing market, the investors are able to benefit from any price increase. The take up rate of the EPS will be an indicator of the quality of the government of the day. Additionally, there is a high level of transparency required of the government, as the proceeds cannot be spent elsewhere.

This dimension of accountability ensures the equitable right of the provider of funds. The collective participation creates a positive behavioral impact that achieves the agenda of accountability, transparency, effective governance on the part of the government, and mutual support for projects that qualify as the engine of the nation's growth. This good governance structure is very much needed in today's world, where the effects of debt-based financing is laden with moral hazard and irresponsible financial transactions that benefit only a few parties. Close partnership between the public and the government generates a positive "feel good" factor that can reduce social ills such as corruption, displacement and manipulation of public funds. Instead, it upholds integrity, responsibility, transparency and solidarity among the people and the government.

The issue of government transparency ties up neatly with the point made in previous chapters on tax revenue collection. When the government is transparent with their spending, the taxpayer will be more willing to pay their taxes as they know where and how their money is being spent. This is similar to an act of charitable contributions that people make. They feel good about making a charitable contribution as they know that the money is going towards a good cause. If good governance is practiced, taxpayers will have less incentive to shirk tax payments.

6.7.3 Economic Resilience

With less strain on debt levels and the option of an alternative source of funding from private sector savings, the government could then undertake more development projects that will generate GDP growth for the country. With better transparency, only the most viable projects that benefit the country's citizens will be undertaken.

The risk-sharing feature of public sector financing will forge a much closer connection between the country's financial and real sectors, thus imparting greater stability and resilience to the economy. There will be better alignment of the financial and real sector as the rate of return on the EPS is benchmarked against the rate of return of the development project or the rate of return of the economy. This is an ex-post return, which mirrors closely the performance of the project rather than a predetermined rate of return as is applicable in a debt-based instrument.

This arrangement will also promote financial inclusion among the majority of the people of Malaysia. The participants can reduce the risk of income volatility and allow consumption smoothing, enhancing the welfare of the state.

6.8 Conclusion

Although empirical analysis has shown that Malaysia's current fiscal policy, with all its shortcomings, is sustainable; the sustainability is not necessarily robust. This means that the economy is exposed to a deteriorating fiscal position if external shocks were to occur, or the expected economic growth is not forthcoming.

Therefore, the book proposes an alternative fiscal framework that comprises a fairer tax structure and interest-free public financing. The aim of the reform in the tax structure is to redistribute wealth and increase tax revenue through greater tax compliance whilst maintaining the simplicity, fairness and participation of everyone in the economy. It is also aimed at inviting public participation in the development of the nation through risk-sharing financing by the government. The sustainability of Malaysia under the proposed fiscal framework was assessed and the empirical results show that fiscal sustainability is stronger under the proposed fiscal framework.

The benefits of the proposed fiscal framework are manifold. The desired result of the whole reform is the equilibrium of competing interests that puts the financial impact outcome in its proper perspective. It not only provides a better fiscal sustainability position, but the policy tools provide an incentive structure for closing the gap between the financial and real sector of the economy, and at the same time enhances rule compliance and social solidarity through the mutual sharing of risks and return that are needed to achieve economic justice. This is where we can refer to the achievement of the characteristics of an economy based on Islamic worldview as mentioned in the first chapter of this book, since the overriding principle in an Islamic economy is the promotion of social justice and equity. The overall positive impact is not only evident in the robustness and sustainability of the economy, but also on the behavior of the government and participants in the economy.

References

Aaberge, R., Colombino, U., & Holmøy, E. (2004). Population Ageing and Fiscal Sustainability: An Integrated Micro-macro Analysis of Required Tax Changes, (367).

Aaberge, R., Colombino, U., & Strøm, S. (2000). Labor Supply Responses and Welfare Effects from Replacing Current Tax Rules by a Flat Tax: Empirical Evidence from Italy, Norway and Sweden. *Journal of Population Economics*.

Abdullah, H., Mustafa, M. M., & Dahalan, J. (2012). An Empirical Study on Fiscal Sustainability in Malaysia. *International Journal of Academic Research in Business and Social Sciences*, *2*(1), 72–90. Retrieved from www.hrmars.com/journals

Adam, S. (2010). *The Theory of Moral Sentiments* (copyright@.). Digireads.comPublishing.

Afonso, A. (2005). Fiscal Sustainability: The Unpleasant European Case. *FinanzArchiv: Public Finance Analysis*, (June). Retrieved from http://www.ingentaconnect.com/content/mohr/fa/2005/00000061/00000001/art00002

Agell, J., & Persson, M. (2001). On the analytics of the dynamic Laffer curve. *Journal of Monetary Economics*, (682). Retrieved from http://www.sciencedirect.com/science/article/pii/S0304393201000745

Ahmad, E., & Best, M. (2012). Financing Social Policy in the Presence of Informality, (March), 1–26.

Ahmad, E., Best, M., & Pöschl, C. (2012). Tax Reforms in the Presence of Informality in Developing Countries Incentives to Cheat in Mexico, (October), 1–33.

Aktas, A., & Tiftik, M. E. (2009). Measuring Fiscal Sustainability for Practical Use in Short-Term Policy Making. Retrieved from http://ecommons.luc.edu/cgi/viewcontent.cgi?article=1104&context=meea

Al-Hasani, B., & Mirakhor, A. (2003). *Iqtisad – The Islamic Approach to Economic Problems*. Global Scholarly Publications.

Alesina, A., & Tabellini, G. (2005). *Why is Fiscal Policy Often Procyclical?* (No. NBER Working Paper No.11600).

Allingham, M. G., & Sandmo, A. (1972). Income Tax Evasion: A Theoretical Analysis. *Journal of Public Economics*, *1*, 323–338.

Alm, J. (1996). What Is An "Optimal" Tax System? *National Tax Journal*, *49* (1). Retrieved from http://www.jstor.org/stable/41789190

Altig, D., Auerbach, A. J., Kotlikoff, L. J., & Smetters, K. A. (2001). Simulating Fundamental Tax Reform in the United States. *American Economic Review*, *91*(3), 574–595.

Angyridis, C. (2013). Endogenous Growth with Public Capital and Progressive Taxation, 1–35. Retrieved from http://economics.soc.uoc.gr/macro/docs/Year/2013/papers/paper_1_59.pdf

Arcand, J., Berkes, E., & Panizza, U. (2012). *Too Much Finance ?* (No. WP/12/161).

Arestis, P., Cipollini, A., & Fattouh, B. (2004). Threshold effects in the U.S. budget deficit. *Economic Inquiry*, *42*(2), 214–222. doi:10.1093/ei/cbh055

Arghyrou, M. G., & Luintel, K. B. (2007). Government solvency: Revisiting some EMU countries. *Journal of Macroeconomics*, *29*(2), 387–410. doi:10.1016/j.jmacro.2005.09.001

Ariff, M. (1998). The Malaysian Economic Experience and Its Relevance for the Oic Member Countries. *Islamic Economic Studies*, *6*(1), 1–41.

Arnold, B. J. (2008). *Do Tax Structures Affect Economic Growth? Empirical Evidence from a Panel of OECD Countries*.

Artis, M., & Marcellino, M. (2000). The Solvency of Government Finances in Europe. *Banca d'Italia*.

Askari, H., Iqbal, Z., Noureddine, K., & Mirakhor, A. (2012). *Risk Sharing in Finance: The Islamic Finance Alternative*. John Wiley & Sons (Asia) Pte Ltd.

Asteriou, D., & Hall, S. G. (2007). *Applied Econometrics: A Modern Approach*. Palgrave Macmillan.

https://doi.org/10.1515/9783110591187-007

Atkinson, A. (1971). Capital taxes, the redistribution of wealth and individual savings. *The Review of Economic Studies*. Retrieved from http://www.jstor.org/stable/10.2307/2296780

Auerbach, A., Kotlikoff, L., & Leibfritz, W. (1998). *Generational Accounting Around the World*. Retrieved from http://www.imes.boj.or.jp/edps98/98-E-02.pdf

Baharumshah, A. Z., & Lau, E. (2007). Regime changes and the sustainability of fiscal imbalance in East Asian countries. *Economic Modelling*, *24*(6), 878–894. doi:10.1016/j.econmod.2007.03.002

Bajo-Rubio, O., Díaz-Roldán, C., & Esteve, V. (2010). On the sustainability of government deficits: Some long-term evidence for spain, 1850–2000. *Journal of Applied Economics*, *13*(2), 263–281. doi:10.1016/S1514-0326(10)60012-8

Bajo-Rubio, O., Díaz-Roldán, C., & Esteve, V. (2004). Searching for threshold effects in the evolution of budget deficits: an application to the Spanish case. *Economics Letters*, *82*(2), 239–243. doi:10.1016/j.econlet.2003.07.010

Balassone, F., & Franco, D. (2000). Assessing Fiscal Sustainability: A Review of Methods with a View to EMU. *Available at SSRN 2109377*, *66*(1944). Retrieved from http://papers.ssrn.com/sol3/papers.cfm?abstract_id=2109377

Barnhill Jr, T. M., & Kopits, G. (2003). *Assessing Fiscal Sustainability Under Uncertainty*.

Barro, R. J. (1979). On the Determination of the Public Debt. *Journal of Political Economy*, *87*(5), 940. doi:10.1086/260807

Bauducco, S., & Caprioli, F. (2014). Optimal fiscal policy in a small open economy with limited commitment. *Journal of International Economics*, *93*(2), 302–315. doi:10.1016/j.jinteco.2014.04.001

Baum, A., Checherita-Westphal, C., & Rother, P. (2013). Debt and Growth : New Evidence for the Euro Area. *Journal of International Money . . .*, *32*, 809–821. Retrieved from http://www.sciencedirect.com/science/article/pii/S0261560612001490

Bezemer, D. (2012). Finance and Growth : When Credit Helps, and When it Hinders, 1–45. Retrieved from http://scholar.google.com/scholar?hl=en&btnG=Search&q=intitle:Finance+and+Growth+:+When+Credit+Helps+,+and+When+it+Hinders#1

Blanchard, O., Chouraqui, J.-C., Hagemann, R. P., & Sartor, N. (1990). *Blanchard (1990) The sustainability of fiscal policy* (No. 15).

Blanchard, O. J. (1990). *Suggestions for a New Set of Fiscal Indicators* (No. 79).

Boadway, R., Chamberlain, E., & Emmerson, C. (2010). Taxation of Wealth and Wealth Transfers. *Dimensions of Tax Design: . . .*. Retrieved from http://www.ifs.org.uk/mirrleesreview/reports/conference_drafts/taxation_wealth.pdf

Bogaert, H. (2000). Long-term Fiscal Sustainability in Belgium. *Banca d'Italia (2000)*. Retrieved from http://papers.ssrn.com/sol3/papers.cfm?abstract_id=2109445

Bohn, H. (1991). On Testing Sustainability of Government Deficits in a Stochastic Environment.

Bohn, H. (2005). *The Sustainability of Fiscal Policy in the United States* (No. 1446).

Bohn, H. (2007). Are stationarity and cointegration restrictions really necessary for the intertemporal budget constraint? *Journal of Monetary Economics*, *54*(7), 1837–1847. doi:10.1016/j.jmoneco.2006.12.012

Browning, E., & Browning, J. (1985). Why Not a True Flat Rate Tax? *Cato J.*, *5*(2), 629–656. Retrieved from http://heinonlinebackup.com/hol-cgi-bin/get_pdf.cgi?handle=hein.journals/catoj5&section=47

Buiter, W. H. (1985). A Guide to Public Sector Debt and Deficits.

Burnside, C. (2004). Assessing New Approaches to Fiscal Sustainability Analysis. *World Bank, Mimeo*, (September). Retrieved from http://citeseerx.ist.psu.edu/viewdoc/download?doi=10.1.1.113.9659&rep=rep1&type=pdf

Caminada, K., & Goudswaard, K. (2010). Distributional Effects of a Flat Tax, An Empirical Analysis for the Netherlands. *Research Memorandum Department*. . ., (20184). Retrieved from http://papers.ssrn.com/sol3/papers.cfm?abstract_id=1436423

Cecchetti, S. G., Mohanty, M. S., & Zampolli, F. (2011). The real effects of debt. *Review of Financial Studies*, *22*(September), 25–27. doi:10.1093/rfs/hhm061

Chalk, N., & Hemming, R. (2000). *Assessing fiscal sustainability in theory and practice* (No. WP/00/81).

Chen, S. W. (2014). Testing for fiscal sustainability: New evidence from the G-7 and some European countries. *Economic Modelling*, *37*, 1–15. doi:10.1016/j.econmod.2013.10.024

Chen, Y. K. (2012). The Progressivity of the Malaysian Personal Income Tax System. *Kajian Malaysia*, *30*(2), 27–43.

Choudhry, N., & Mirakhor, A. (1997). Indirect Instruments of Monetary Control in an Islamic Financial System. *Islamic Economic Studies*, *4* (2). Retrieved from http://www.irti.org/irj/go/km/docs/documents/IDBDevelopments/Internet/English/IRTI/CM/downloads/IES_Articles/Vol4-2.NurunChoudhryandAMirakhor.INDIRECTINSTRUMENTSOFMONETARY.dp.pdf

Clotfelter, C. T. (1983). Tax Evasion and Tax Rates: An Analysis of Individual Returns. *The Review of Economics and Statistics*, *LXV*(3).

Croce, E., & Juan-Ramón, V. (2003). *Assessing Fiscal Sustainability: A Cross Country Comparison* (No. WP/03/145). IMF Working Paper, WP/03/145.

Debrun, X., & Kapoor, R. (2010). Fiscal Policy and Macroeconomic Stability: New Evidence and Policy Implications. *Bank of Italy Occasional Paper*. Retrieved from http://papers.ssrn.com/sol3/papers.cfm?abstract_id=1985197

DeLong, J., & Summers, L. (2012). Fiscal Policy in a Depressed Economy. . . . *Papers on Economic* . . ., 1–52. Retrieved from http://www.jstor.org/stable/23287218

Diamond, P., & Saez, E. (2011). The Case for a Progressive Tax: From Basic Research to Policy Recommendations. *The Journal of Economic Perspectives*. Retrieved from http://www.ingentaconnect.com/content/aea/jep/2011/00000025/00000004/art00008

Dickey, B. Y. D. a, & Fuller, W. a. (1981). Likelihood Ratio Statistics for Autoregressive Time Series with a Unit Root. *Econometrica*, *49*(4), 1057–1072. doi:10.2307/1912517

Dickey, D. A., & Fuller, W. A. (1979). Distribution of the estimators for autoregressive time series with a unit root. *Journal of the American Statistical Association*, *74*(366), 427–431.

Domar, E. D. (1944). The Burdern of the Debt and the National Income. *The American Economic Review*, *34*(4), 798–827. doi:10.1126/science.151.3712.867-a

Duncan, D., & Peter, K. S. (2008). *Tax Progressivity and Income Inequality* (No. 08-26).

Duncan, D., & Peter, K. S. (2012). Unequal Inequalities: Do Progressive Taxes Reduce Income Inequality?, (6910). Retrieved from http://www.econstor.eu/handle/10419/67217

Ebb, T. (2004). *Wealth Tax in Europe : Why the Decline?* (Vol. 33).

Ehrhart, H., Minea, A., & Villieu, P. (2009). Deficit, Seigniorage and the Growth Laffer Curve in developing countries.

Elliot, G., Rothenberg, T. J., & Stock, J. H. (1996). Efficient tests for autoregressive unit root. *Econometrica*, *64*(4), 813–836.

Elmendorf, D., & Mankiw, N. G. (1999). Government debt. *Handbook of Macroeconomics*. Retrieved from http://www.sciencedirect.com/science/article/pii/S1574004899100387

Engle, R. F., & Granger, C. W. J. (1987). Co-integration and Error Correction: Representation, Estimation, and Testing. *Econometrica*, *55*(2), 251–76. doi:http://dx.doi.org/10.2307/1913236

Escario, R., Gadea, M. D., & Sabaté, M. (2012). Multicointegration, seigniorage and fiscal sustainability. Spain 1857–2000. *Journal of Policy Modeling*, *34*(2), 270–283. doi:10.1016/j.jpolmod.2011.09.001

European Commission. (2006). European Economy. *No 3/2006*, (December).

Marinheiro, C. (2006). The Sustainability of Portuguese Fiscal Policy from a Historical Perspective. *Empirica*. Retrieved from http://link.springer.com/article/10.1007/s10663-006-9013-0

Martin, G. M. (2000). US deficit sustainability: A new approach based on multiple endogenous breaks. *Journal of Applied Econometrics of Applied*, *15*(1), 83–105.

Mcdonnell, T. A. (2013). Wealth Tax: Options for its Implementatin in the Republic of Ireland, (6).

Mendoza, E., & Oviedo, P. (2004). Fiscal solvency and macroeconomic uncertainty in emerging markets: the tale of the tormented insurer. *Econometric Society*, (June). Retrieved from http://www.perjacobsson.org/external/np/res/seminars/2004/60/pdf/mendoz.pdf

Miners, S. (2000). Long-term fiscal projections: Assessing sustainability in the United Kingdom. *Fiscal Sustainability Conference*, *7*. Retrieved from http://papers.ssrn.com/sol3/papers.cfm?abstract_id=2109454

Mirakhor, A. (1993). Equilibrium in a non-interest open economy. *Journal of King Abdulaziz University*, *5*(1), 3–23. Retrieved from http://ceh.njb.kau.edu.sa/Files/320/Researches/50879_21016.pdf

Mirakhor, A. (2010). Whither Islamic Finance? Risk Sharing in An Age of Crises. In *Inaugural Securities Comission Malaysia – Oxford Centre for Islamic Studies Roundtable* (pp. 1–29).

Mirakhor, A. (2011). Risk Sharing and Public Policy. In *5th International Islamic Capital Market Forum, securities Commission of Malaysia*. Kuala Lumpur, Malaysia.

Mirakhor, A. (2012). Shariah Compliant Macro-Economic Policy. *Ifikr.isra.my*, (November). Retrieved from http://ifikr.isra.my/documents/10180/16168/keynote-ProfAbbasIF, RiskSharingandMacroeconomicPolicies.pdf.

Mirakhor, A., & Zaidi, I. (1991). Stabilisation and growth in an open Islamic economy. *Review of Islamic Economics*, *1*(2), 1–20.

Miyazaki, T. (2014). Fiscal reform and fiscal sustainability: Evidence from Australia and Sweden. *International Review of Economics and Finance*, *33*, 141–151. doi:10.1016/j.iref.2014.04.002

Moreno-Dodson, B. (2013). *Is Fiscal Policy the Answer?: A Developing Country Perspective*. (B. Moreno-Dodson, Ed.)*Vasa*. International Bank for Reconstuction and Development/The World Bank.

Mundle, S., Bhanumurthy, N. R., & Das, S. (2011). Fiscal consolidation with high growth: A policy simulation model for India. *Economic Modelling*, *28*(6), 2657–2668. doi:10.1016/j.econmod.2011.08.001

Musgrave, R. (1966). Principles of budget determination. *In: Cameron,H, Handerson, W (Eds), Public Finance: Selected Readings. Random House, New York*, 15–27.

Neaime, S. (2015). Sustainability of budget deficits and public debts in selected European Union countries. *The Journal of Economic Asymmetries*, *12*(1), 1–21. doi:10.1016/j.jeca.2014.10.002

OECD, E. D. P. N. N. 1. (2012). What are the Best Policy Instruments for Fiscal Consolidation?, (12).

Omar, M. A., Noor, A. M., & Meera, A. K. M. (2010). Islamic Pricing Benchmark. *International Shari'ah Research Academy for Islamic Finance Research Paper No 16/2010*, 1–85.

Ostry, M., Berg, M., & Tsangarides, M. (2014). *Redistribution, Inequality, and Growth*. Retrieved from http://books.google.com/books?hl=en&id=i2ccAwAAQBAJ&oi=fnd&pg=PP1&dq=Redistribution+,+Inequality+,+and+Growth&ots=_s6rlAlkrt&sig=6arty5Y4yhzzT1nq_8rZzWjEbfA

Othman, A., & Mirakhor, A. (2013). Islam and Development: Policy Challenges. In Z. I. and A. Mirakhor (Ed.), *Economic Development and Islamic Finance*. World Bank Publications.

Palil, M. R., & Ibrahim, M. A. (2011). The Impacts Of Goods And Services Tax (GST) On Middle Income Earners In Malaysia, *1*(3), 192–206.

Palil, M. R., & Mustapha, A. F. (2011). Determinants of Tax Compliance in Asia : A case of Malaysia. *European Journal of Social Sciences*, *24*(1).

Paulus, A., & Peichl, A. (2008). Effects of Flat Tax Reforms in Western Europe on Equity and Efficiency. *FiFo-CPE Discussion Paper*. Retrieved from http://papers.ssrn.com/sol3/papers.cfm?abstract_id=1106173

Perotti, R. (1999). Fiscal policy in good times and bad. *The Quarterly Journal of Economics*, 1–43. Retrieved from http://qje.oxfordjournals.org/content/114/4/1399.short
Perotti, R., & Alesina, A. (1995). Fiscal expansions and fiscal adjustments in OECD countries, (754). Retrieved from http://www.nber.org/papers/w5214
Pescatori, A., Sandri, D., & Simon, J. (2014). Debt and Growth: Is There a Magic Threshold? *IMF Working Papers*, *14*(34), 1. doi:10.5089/9781484306444.001
Phillips, P. c b, & Perron, P. (1988). Testing for a unit root in time series regression. *Biometrica*, *75* (2), 335–46.
Piketty, T. (2014). *Capital in the Twenty-First Century*. Belknap Press.
Polito, V., & Wickens, M. (2012). A model-based indicator of the fiscal stance. *European Economic Review*, *56*(3), 526–551. doi:10.1016/j.euroecorev.2011.12.003
Polito, V., & Wickens, M. R. (2005). Measuring Fiscal Sustainability. *Discussion Paper Series-Centre for Economic Policy Research London*, *44* (0),ALL. Retrieved from http://www.st-andrews.ac.uk/economics/CDMA/papers/cp0503.pdf
Quintos, C. E. (1995). Sustainability of the deficit process with structural shifts. *Journal of Business and Economic Statistics*, *13*(4), 409–417.
Rafiq, S., & Zeufack, A. (2012). *Fiscal Multipliers over the Growth Cycle: Evidence from Malaysia* (No. 5982). *World Bank Policy Research Working Paper*. Retrieved from http://papers.ssrn.com/sol3/papers.cfm?abstract_id=2016747
Ragayah, H. M. Z. (2010). Understanding the Formulation of the Revised Poverty Line in Malaysia. *Akademika*, *70*, 21–39.
Rajan, R. G. (2010). *Fault Lines: How Hidden Fractures Still Threaten the World Economy*. Princeton University Press.
Ranciere, R., & Kumhof, M. (2010). *Inequality, leverage and crises*. Retrieved from http://books.google.com/books?hl=en&id=lPpMOR387eQC&oi=fnd&pg=PA3&dq=Inequality+,+Leverage+and+Crises&ots=tsmEOe4I3m&sig=WRp5ipe5cZGUtKSTRE4viVY3A4U
Reinhart, C. M., Reinhart, V. R., & Rogoff, K. S. (2012a). *Debt Overhangs: Past and Present* (No. 18015) (Vol. 3). Retrieved from http://www.nber.org/papers/w18015
Reinhart, C. M., Reinhart, V. R., & Rogoff, K. S. (2012b). Public Debt Overhangs: Advanced-Economy Episodes Since 1800. *Journal of Economic Perspectives*, *26*(3), 69–86. doi:10.1257/jep.26.3.69
Reinhart, C. M., & Rogoff, K. S. (2009). *This Time is Different: Eight Centuries of Financial Follies*. Pinceton University Press.
Reinhart, C. M., & Rogoff, K. S. (2010). Growth in a Time of Debt. *American Economic Review*, *100*(2), 573–578. doi:10.1257/aer.100.2.573
Reinhart, C., & Rogoff, K. (2009). *This Time is Different: Eight Centuries of Financial Folly*. Princeton University Press.
Røed, K., & Strøm, S. (2002). Progressive Taxes and the Labour Market: Is the Trade–off Between Equality and Efficiency Inevitable? *Journal of Economic Surveys*, *16*(1), 77–110. Retrieved from http://onlinelibrary.wiley.com/doi/10.1111/1467-6419.00160/abstract
Rogoff, K. S. (2011). Global Imbalances Without Tears. *Project Syndicate*, *2011-03-01*.
Salih, K., Hwok-Aun, L., & Khalid, M. A. (2014). *Malaysian Human Development Report 2013 – Redesigning an Inclusive Future*.
Salti, N. (2011). Income Inequality and the Composition of Public Debt. In *Politics and Economic Development ERF 17th Annual Conference*.
Sari, N., & Mirakhor, A. (2012). Islamic Monetary Policy in Malaysia: A Conceptual Framework. *Ifikr.isra.my*, (November). Retrieved from http://ifikr.isra.my/documents/10180/16168/e1-NorhanimIslamicMonetoryPolicy.pdf
Sarno, L. (2001). The behavior of US public debt: a nonlinear perspective. *Economics Letters*, *74*(1), 119–125. doi:10.1016/S0165-1765(01)00529-8

Shakow, D., & Shuldiner, R. (1999). *A Comprehensive Wealth Tax* (No. 266). *Tax L. Rev.* Retrieved from http://heinonlinebackup.com/hol-cgi-bin/get_pdf.cgi?handle=hein.journals/taxlr53&section=26

Shiller, R. (2003). *The new financial order: Risk in the 21st century*. Princeton University Press.

Shiller, R. (2009). *The new financial order: Risk in the 21st century*. Retrieved from http://net.educause.edu/ir/library/pdf/ff0610S.pdf

Slemrod, J., & Yitzhaki, S. (2002). Tax Avoidance, Evasion, and Administration, *3*. Retrieved from http://www.sciencedirect.com/science/article/pii/S157344200280026X

Smith, A. (1776). *An Inquiry into the Nature and Causes of the Wealth of Nations*. (E. Cannan, Ed.). Methuen & Co, London 1904.

Stock, J. H., & Watson, M. W. (1993). A simple estimation of cointegrating vectors in higher order integrated systems. *Econometrica*, *61*, 783–820. Retrieved from http://search.ebscohost.com/login.aspx?direct=true&db=bth&AN=12149864&site=ehost-live&scope=site

Sutherland, D., Hoeller, P., & Merola, R. (2012). Fiscal Consolidation: Part 1. How Much is Needed and How to Reduce Debt to a Prudent Level?, (11). Retrieved from http://papers.ssrn.com/sol3/papers.cfm?abstract_id=1985994

Tabandeh, R., Jusoh, M., Nor, N. G. M., & Zaidi, M. A. S. (2012). Estimating Factors Affecting Tax Evasion in Malaysia : A Neural Network Method Analysis. In *Persidangan Kebangsaan Ekonomi Malaysia ke VII (PERKEM VII)* (Vol. 2, pp. 1524–1535). Ipoh, Perak.

Taha, R., & Loganathan, N. (2008). Causality between tax revenue and government spending in malaysia. *The International Journal of Business and Finance Research*, *2*(2), 63–73. Retrieved from http://ssrn.com/abstract=1543911

Tanner, E. (2013). *Fiscal Sustainability : A 21 st Century Guide for the Perplexed* (No. WP/12/89).

Trabandt, M., & Uhlig, H. (2011). The Laffer Curve Revisited. *Journal of Monetary Economics*, *58*(4), 305–327. doi:10.1016/j.jmoneco.2011.07.003

Tran-nam, B. B. (2000). The Implementation Costs of the GST in Australia : Concepts, Preliminary Estimates and Implications. *Journal of Australian Taxation*, (July), 331–343.

Trehan, B., & Walsh, C. E. (1988). Common trends, the government's budget constraint, and revenue smoothing. *Journal of Economic Dynamics and Control*, *12*(2–3), 425–444. doi:10.1016/0165-1889(88)90048-6

Trehan, B., & Walsh, C. E. (1991). Testing Intertemporal Budget Constraints: Theory and Application to U.S. Federal Budget and Current Account Deficits. *Journal of Money, Credit and Banking*, *23* (2), 206–223.

Uctum, M., Thurston, T., & Uctum, R. (2006). Public Debt, the Unit Root Hypothesis and Structural Breaks: A Multi-Country Analysis. *Economica*, (June). Retrieved from http://onlinelibrary.wiley.com/doi/10.1111/j.1468-0335.2006.00451.x/full

Ul Haque, N., & Mirakhor, A. (1999). The Design of Instruments for Government Finance in an Islamic Economy. *Islamic Economic Studies*, *6*(2), 27–43.

Voinea, L., & Mihaescu, F. (2009). The impact of the flat tax reform on inequality. The case of Romania. *Romanian Journal of Economic Forecasting*, 19–41. Retrieved from http://mail.ipe.ro/rjef/rjef4_09/rjef4_09_2.pdf

Wyplosz, C. (2012). *Fiscal Rules: Theoretical Issues and Historical Experience* (No. 17884). Retrieved from http://www.nber.org/papers/w17884

Zhou, L. Z., Jarren, T., & Heng-Contaxis Jordon. (2013). The Introduction Of Goods And Services Tax In Malaysia : A Policy Analysis.

Zivot, E., & Andrews, D. W. K. (1992). Further Evidence on the Great Crash, the Oil Price Shock and the Unt Root Hypothesis. *Journal of Business and Economic Statistics*, *10*(3).

List of Figures

https://doi.org/10.1515/9783110591187-008

List of Tables

https://doi.org/10.1515/9783110591187-009

Appendix A Implementation of GST in Malaysia

Currently, there are two Acts that separately govern the goods and services known as Sales Tax Act 1972 and Service Tax Act 1975 (the SST), which is under the purview of the Royal Malaysian Customs and Excise Department (the Customs). Sales tax is imposed on a consumer who consumes taxable goods, which is then collected by business enterprises and made accountable to the Customs. Service tax on the other hand is imposed on a consumer who consumes foods or services; for example, places such as hotels, health centers or professional services such as auditing firm and such other services as listed under the Second Schedule of the Service Tax Regulations 1975. Basically, both sales and services tax are single stage tax levied on consumers at the consumption stage. It is known as a single stage tax due to the fact that tax is charged only once, either at the input or output stage.

GST, on the other hand, is a multi-stage tax. As a value-added tax, payments are made at every stage of production and distribution through to the final consumer. However, under the GST the tax chargeable on non-capital inputs are claimable, or eligible for refund. Therefore, the tax burden is passed on to customers at the point of purchase. In contrast, the current sales tax is imposed on the manufacturer, before the services tax is imposed on the consumer at the point of purchase. One cited advantage of the GST is that it is a self-policing mechanism, as businesses automatically factor in the GST as part of the selling price on inputs to other manufacturers. This indirectly administers the imposition of the GST, while significantly reducing cases of tax avoidance. Businesses know that the GST is claimable and have less incentive to evade tax. By transferring the tax burden from manufacturers to consumers, the cost of doing business is further reduced and the gains should (in theory) be passed on to consumers through lower prices.

In Malaysia, the introduction of GST is aimed at improving revenue collection and reducing the nation's growing budget deficit. Apart from political considerations, there are many factors involved in the deferment of GST; the foremost is the readiness issue among small and medium-sized enterprises. Many businesses have realized that GST preparation is complex and will have a profound impact on financial reporting and strategic decisions in many areas of business including business planning, pricing and competitive positions. In addition, businesses projected high initial costs especially for the establishment of an effective information system and knowledgeable team for GST operation. This will include computerization, electronic filing facilities, education and training and employment of specialized experts to handle GST matters. GST in Malaysia was implemented at a rate of 6% (2% higher than initially expected). The rate is seen as high for an implementation stage, compared to 3% imposed by Singapore when they first introduced GST, and considering the problem of high cost of living currently surrounding the Malaysian population.

https://doi.org/10.1515/9783110591187-010

Mechanism of GST: Under the GST environment, the tax imposed is divided into two categories, namely input tax and output tax.

1. Input tax – Input tax is the GST that a taxable person incurs on the purchase of goods and services in the course or furtherance of his business.
2. Output tax – Output tax is the GST that a taxable person charges on his taxable supply of goods and services made by him in the course or furtherance of his business.

A taxable product or service may fall under one of the three categories of GST rates: standard-rated supplies, zero-rated supplies and exempt supplies. The tax treatments for these different categories are different as explained below.

1. Standard-rated supplies – These are defined as taxable supply of goods and services, which are subject to a standard rate. The taxable person is eligible to claim input tax credit on his business inputs in making taxable supplies.
2. Zero-rated supplies – These are taxable supplies, which are subject to a zero rate. Although there is no GST to be imposed on these supplies, the taxable person is eligible to claim input tax credit on his business inputs in making taxable supplies.
3. Exempt supplies – These are non-taxable supplies that are not subject to GST. Suppliers of exempt supplies are not eligible to claim the GST incurred on his business inputs.

Figure Apx. 1 illustrates the difference between taxes collected under the different categories of GST.

For exempt supplies, wholesalers or retailers will be the bearer of the GST. As GST is supposed to be tax neutral to businesses, the exempt supplies may create an additional cost to them. In this respect, a fixed input tax recovery mechanism is put in place whereby the affected businesses are eligible to claim a predetermined amount of input tax from Customs. However, in some situation, the amount recoverable from Customs may not be the full amount of tax suffered.

GST is said to be better than the current SST as it eliminates the double tax along the value-chain which pushes prices up, meaning that the cost of doing business will drop. But, how much of these savings would translate into cheaper products and services? Businesses that are eligible for GST claims may not reduce their selling price. At the same time, how much of the cost suffered from exempt supplies and cost of implementation of GST will be passed on to customers? GST may be too costly for small traders to implement. To claim input tax, they have to be registered and comply with the required tax returns. Penalty provisions put in place are quite hefty that small traders may decide to absorb the input tax and passed on this cost to customers in terms of increased prices. The onus will then fall on consumers to compare prices and allow the market forces to keep businesses' price competitive. The Anti-Profiteering Act, introduced to combat profiteering activities, assumes a

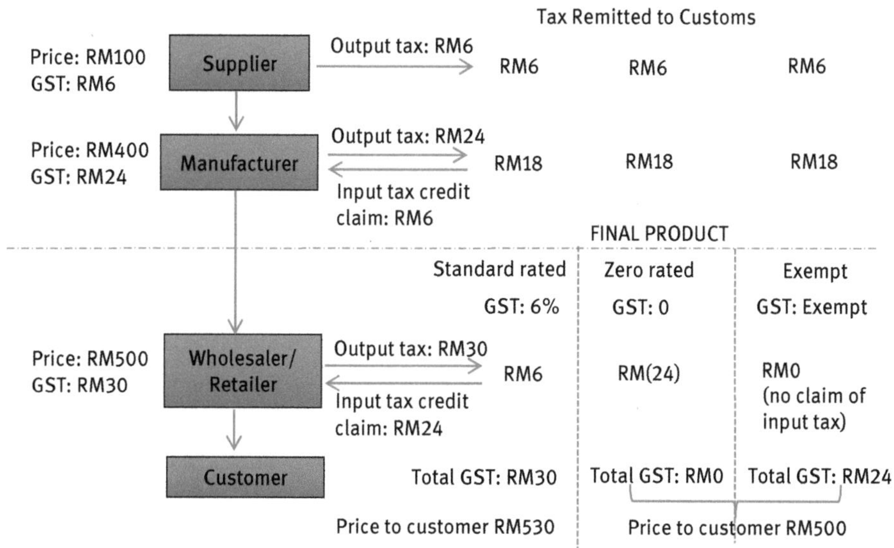

Figure Apx. 1: Taxes collected under the different categories of GST.

high level of efficiency on the part of enforcement agencies to carry out their duties. Poor and rural households are more susceptible to price manipulation. Price competition is less intense in rural areas due to the smaller number of business establishments as well as low level of awareness of consumer rights.

The issue of regressivity inherent in GST remains a major concern. Even though exemptions can be given on many basic necessities, tax is now imposed on a wider range of products and services than under the SST system. This means additional costs on most goods and services for low-income household and the rich alike. The GST will put upward pressure on cost of living through inflation during the initial stages. Having almost two third of the population falling under the low- and middle-income category, the implementation of GST will naturally put further financial stress on Malaysian households.

Having said that, GST has the advantage of detecting tax evaders. The informal economy workers, such as roadside vendors and part-time workers will now fall under the GST net. The GST net also captures tax from unethical evasion and tax avoidance activities. Illegal activities such as embezzlement and smuggling will, at some level, be indirectly subjected to GST. If the GST is efficiently implemented, it will be a blanket that covers the majority of the economy. This represents an even larger responsibility on the part of the government to adhere to moral values and spend prudently.

Appendix B Sources of Data

Table Apx 1: Data Used and Sources of Data.

Data	Years	Source/Remarks
Gross Domestic Product (*Y*)	1970–2013	World Bank Database
Real GDP Growth (*g*)	1970–2013	World Bank Database
Government Debt (*D*)	1970–2020	Bank Negara Monthly Statistical Bulletin (various issues) Note: This is total government debt including external debts
Government Revenue (*R*)	1970–2020	Bank Negara Monthly Statistical Bulletin (various issues) Note: This is federal government tax and non-tax revenue
Government Expenditure (*GG*) Surplus/Deficit to GDP Debt to GDP Individual Savings	1970–2020 1970–2020 1970–2020 1970–2020	Bank Negara Monthly Statistical Bulletin (various issues) Note: This is federal government expenditure including interest payment on government debt Tradingeconomics IMF World Economic Outlook 2020 Bank Negara Monthly Statistical Bulletin (various issues)
Primary Surplus/(Deficit) *PS/(PD)*	1970–2013	Own working based on data from Bank Negara Monthly Statistical Bulletin (various issues) Primary Surplus = Government Revenue – Government Development Expenditure – Government Operating Expenditure (excluding Interest on Debt) Note: Data for interest on debt (debt service) for 1970 to 1975 is an estimation based on the average increase in debt service over the years 1976 to 2012
Real Interest Rate (*r*)	1970–2013	World Bank Database Note: Real Interest Rate for 1980 to 1986 is estimated by taking average lending rate and deducting inflation rate (measured by GDP deflator). Due to lack of information on average lending rate, the deposit lending rate is used for 1970 to 1979
Inflation (π)	1970–2013	World Bank Database
Debt Service (Interest on Government Debts) (*ip*)	1970–2013	Bank Negara Monthly Statistical Bulletin (various issues)

https://doi.org/10.1515/9783110591187-011

Table Apx 1 (continued)

Data	Years	Source/Remarks
Interest rate on Government Debts (i)	1970–2013	The average rate of interest on government debt is calculated based on data on interest payment on government debts and government debts from Bank Negara Monthly Statistical Bulletin (various issues).
GDP Deflator	1970–2013	World Bank Database
Target debt-to-GDP ratio (d^*)	N/A	Lowest value reached by the debt ratio during period under review
Discount factor that would prevail once convergence to d^* (β^*)	N/A	Sample mean of the distribution of the observed values of β

Appendix C Derivation of Fiscal Sustainability Index

The government budget for period t is:

$$G + (1+i)D_{t-1} = D_t + R \qquad \text{(i)}$$

where D is the stock of debts, G is government expenditure, R is government revenue and i is interest rate on government debts. The left-hand side represents the total expenditure that is the government expenditure and interest expenses on existing debts and the right-hand side represents total revenue comprising the revenue of the government and borrowing to finance the expenditure. Expressing (i) in terms of primary deficit $PD_t = G_t - R_t$ will give:

$$PD_t = G_t - R_t = D_t - (1+i)D_{t-1} \qquad \text{(ii)}$$

Multiply (ii) by -1 to express (ii) in terms of PS_t :

$$-PD_t = (1+i)D_{t-1} - D_t = iD_{t-1} - (D_t - D_{t-1}) \qquad \text{(iii)}$$

$$\boldsymbol{PS_t = iD_{t-1} - (D_t - D_{t-1})} \qquad \text{(iv)/}\mathbf{(2)}$$

Dividing both sides of the above equation by Y_t (nominal GDP at time t) and defining $d_t = \frac{D_t}{Y_t}$ and $ps_t = \frac{PS_t}{Y_t}$ as well as rearranging the terms, the equation becomes:

$$ps_t + d_t = (1+i)d_{t-1}\left(\frac{Y_{t-1}}{Y_t}\right) \qquad \text{(v)}$$

Expressing the change in the nominal gross domestic product in terms of the growth rate of the real GDP (g) and the inflation rate (π) as $\frac{Y_t}{Y_{t-1}} = (1+\pi_t)(1+g_t)$ will give:

$$ps_t + d_t = \left(\frac{1+i}{(1+\pi_t)(1+g_t)}\right)d_{t-1} \qquad \text{(vi)}$$

By defining the real interest rate as $r_t = \frac{(1+i_t)}{(1+\pi_t)} - 1$, the above equation can be re-written as:

$$d_t = \frac{(1+r_t)}{(1+g)}d_{t-1} - ps_t \qquad \text{(vii)}$$

Defining $\beta_t = \frac{(1+r_t)}{(1+g)}$, we obtain equation (3)

$$\boldsymbol{d_t = \beta_t d_{t-1} - ps_t} \qquad \text{(vii)/}\mathbf{(3)}$$

https://doi.org/10.1515/9783110591187-012

Alternatively, the law of motion for d_t can be expressed as:

$$d_t = \frac{1}{\beta_{t+1}} d_{t+1} + \frac{1}{\beta_{t+1}} ps_{t+1} \tag{viii}$$

Iterating the above equation forward up to time N, will give:

$$d_t = \sum_{s=1}^{N} \frac{ps_{t+s}}{\prod_{k=1}^{s} \beta_{t+k}} + \frac{d_{t+N}}{\prod_{k=1}^{N} \beta_{t+k}} \tag{ix}$$

In special case where $\beta_s = \beta$ and $ps_s = ps$ for all $s \in [t+1,\ t+N]$, the above equation becomes:

$$d_t = ps \sum_{s=1}^{N} \left(\frac{1}{\beta_s}\right) + \frac{d_{t+N}}{\beta^N} = ps \frac{\left(1+\beta^N\right)}{\beta^N (1-\beta)} + \frac{d_{t+N}}{\beta^N} \tag{x}$$

or as expressed in equation (4);

$$\boldsymbol{d_t = \beta^{-1}\, ps_{t+1} + \beta^{-2}\, ps_{t+2} + \ldots + \beta^{-N}\, ps_{t+N} + \beta^{-N}\, d_{t+N}} \qquad \text{(xi)/}\mathbf{(4)}$$

Equation (xi)/(4) above establishes the formal condition for solvency that is the public sector is solvent when the present discounted value of future primary surpluses is equal to the value of the outstanding stock of debt. That means $d_{t+N} = 0$. A less stringent condition is for $d_{t+N} = d^*$, where $0<d^*<d_t$, which means the present value of expected primary surplus ratios will reduce the debt ratio below the current level. The fiscal sustainability indicator proposed is akin to this concept.

Having established the solvency condition, the indicator is derived from the following equations:

$$\boldsymbol{d_t = \beta_t d_{t-1} - ps_t} \qquad \text{(xii)/}\mathbf{(3)}$$

$$\boldsymbol{ps^* = (\beta^* - 1) d^*} \tag{5}$$

$$\boldsymbol{ps_t = ps^* + \lambda_t\ (d_{t-1} - d^*)} \tag{6}$$

where d_t and d^* are the debt-to-GDP ratio and target debt-to-GDP ratio respectively, β_t is the discount factor and β^* is the target discount factor that would prevail once convergence to the target debt ratio, d^* is attained. Equation (5) simply states the primary surplus ratio and the discount factor that would prevail once convergence to the target debt ratio. Equation (6) decomposes the primary surplus into (i) the primary surplus ratio (ps^*) associated with the target debt ratio and (ii) the policy response to the gap between the observed debt ratio and the target debt ratio. λ_t indicates the intensity of the policy response at time t given the debt-ratio gap in the previous period. λ_t is represented by $\frac{ps_t - ps^*}{d_{t-1} - d^*}$ where ps_t is the primary surplus-to-GDP and ps^* is the targeted ratio.

Substituting equations (3) and (5) into equation (6) will give:

$$d_t = \beta_t d_{t-1} - (\beta^* - 1)d^* + \lambda_t(d_{-1} - d_t) \qquad \text{(xiii)}$$

$$\boldsymbol{d_t = (\beta_t - \lambda_t)d_{t-1} - (\beta^* - \lambda_t - 1)d^*} \qquad \text{(xiv)/}\mathbf{(8a)}$$

Equation (8a) states that if the debt ratio at time *t-1* is higher than the target debt ratio, d_t would converge to d^* if and only if $(\beta_t - \lambda_t) < 1$. Therefore, the fiscal sustainability indicator (FSI) is $(\beta_t - \lambda_t)$, where:

$$\boldsymbol{FSI_t = (\beta_t - \lambda_t) = \left(\frac{1 + r_t}{1 + g_t} - \frac{ps_t - ps^*}{d_{t-1} - d^*}\right)} \qquad \text{(xv)/}\mathbf{(8b)}$$

If $d_{t-1} > d^*$, d_t would converge to d^* if and only if $|\beta_t - \lambda_t| < 1$. As such, value of FSI_t below 1 indicates a sustainable fiscal position while values consistently above or equal to 1 indicate unsustainability (Croce & Juan-Ramón, 2003).

Appendix D Islamic Worldview of the Economy

Briefly, the Islamic worldview aims to achieve the following in an economy:
- Social justice and equity – Man has been vested with "free will" and in exercising his freedom of choice, he has to abide to the rules prescribed in Islam which among others is to avoid actions that have conflicting interest to that of the society. This means among others, looking after the needs of the less fortunate and redeeming their rights through income redistribution.
- Trust and transparency – all transactions are anchored through contracts where all parties are aware of their obligations and abide to the rules. Clear and secure property rights, contract enforcement, and trust among people and between people and the government can reduce risk and uncertainty, strengthen social solidarity, and bring private and public interests into harmony.
- Cooperation and coordination through sharing of risks – sharing of risks can cushion the society against adverse consequences of risk occurrence and mitigates uncertainties of life. Sharing of risk intensifies human interaction and increases solidarity among members of the society. The rich in the society are mandated to share the risk of life with the poor, which will decrease the disparity of income in society.
- More equitable distribution of income – distributive justice means there exists a superior distribution of income and wealth in accordance with the universally accepted norms of fairness and equal opportunity for all. Promotion of growth should also aim at maintaining inter-generational equity without favour to the rich minority over an impoverished majority. It also encourages circulation of wealth to ensure the economic ability of the poor grows over time.
- Finance grounded in the real economy – through the use of risk sharing financial instruments, the risk is spread among a large number of participants. The rate of return on these instruments is tied to the performance of the real sector of the economy hence closer coordination between the financial and real sector is promoted.

The role of the state from an Islamic worldview is to ensure that everyone has equal access to resources and means of livelihood, the markets are supervised such that justice is attained and transfers takes place from the more able to the less able – and that distributive justice is ensured for the next generation (Al-Hasani & Mirakhor, 2003).

https://doi.org/10.1515/9783110591187-013

About the Author

Dr. Azura Othman FCCA, C.A(M), CPIF

Azura is a chartered accountant with great passion for Islamic finance and its development. Possessing 19 years of technical and management work experience in top accounting firms of which the last six years was focused on Islamic finance related consultancy work, and 5 years in a professional standard setting body.

She graduated with a degree in Accounting and Finance from the London School of Economics and Political Science, University of London. She is a Fellow of ACCA (UK), a member of Malaysian Institute of Accountant and a chartered member of the Chartered Institute of Islamic Finance Professionals (CIIF). She received her PhD in Islamic Finance from the International Centre of Education in Islamic Finance (INCEIF).

Azura started her career as a Tax Consultant. She was a former Executive Director of PricewaterhouseCoopers Taxation Services, Malaysia with over 19 years of experience, handling tax compliance matters of clients in various sectors and specializing in tax advisory for the financial services industry. She has extensive experience in engagements relating to Islamic Finance, working together with the Malaysian Ministry of Finance, Inland Revenue and the Central Bank. Among her major assignments include working with the Central Bank in formulating the tax incentives for Malaysia as the International Islamic Financial Centre (MIFC) and matters relating to tax neutrality in Islamic Finance.

Currently, Azura is the Chief Executive Officer of the Chartered Institute of Islamic Finance Professionals (CIIF), a professional standard setting body for Islamic finance practitioners. She is also an Independent Non-Executive Director of Malaysia Debt Ventures Berhad (chairman of its Board Audit Committee), Independent Board Member of CIMB Islamic Berhad and a member of the Board of Trustee of Petronas Foundation. She had also served as an Independent Non-Executive Director of Bank Muamalat Malaysia Berhad (an Islamic bank) from 2015 until September 2020, where she chaired the Board Audit Committee and the Nomination and Remuneration Committee. She co-authored a book titled "Macroeconomic Policy and Islamic Finance in Malaysia" as well as various chapters of a book and articles in taxation and Islamic finance.

https://doi.org/10.1515/9783110591187-014

Index

https://doi.org/10.1515/9783110591187-015

Bei Fragen zur Produktsicherheit wenden Sie sich bitte an:
If you have any questions regarding product safety,
please contact:

Walter de Gruyter GmbH
Genthiner Straße 13
10785 Berlin
productsafety@degruyterbrill.com